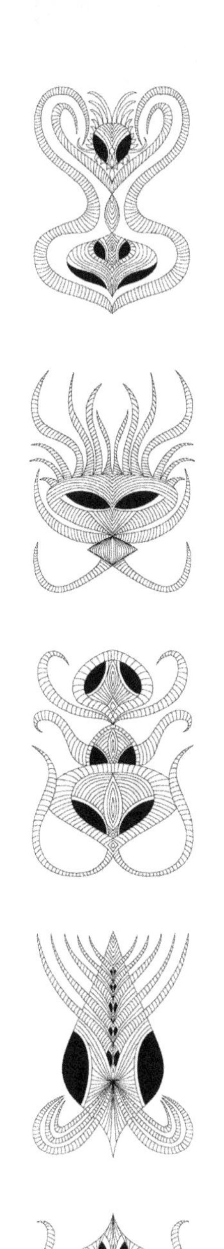
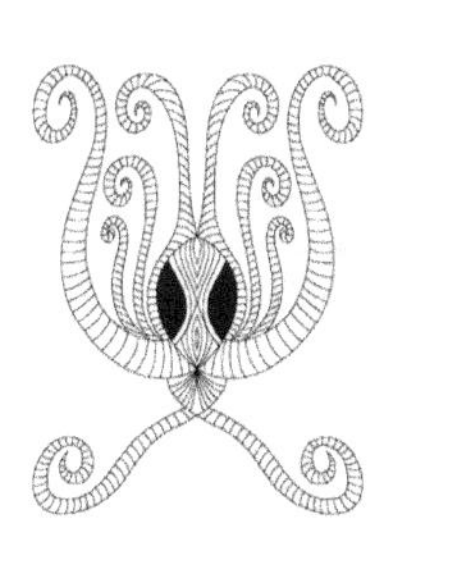
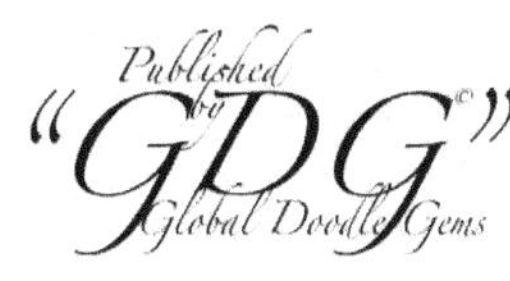

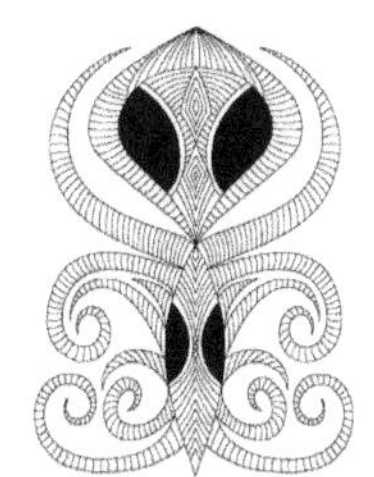

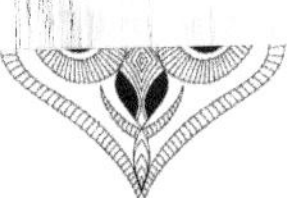
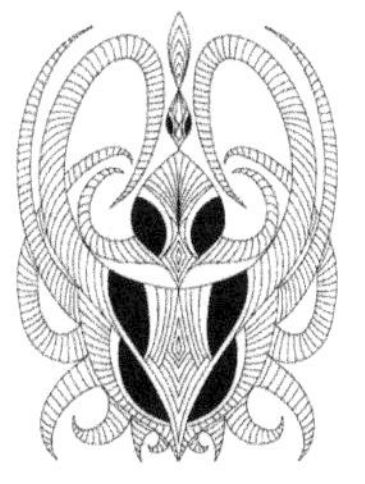
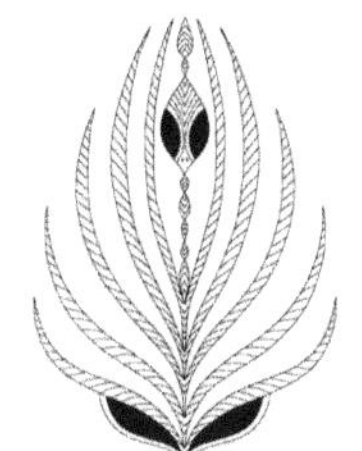
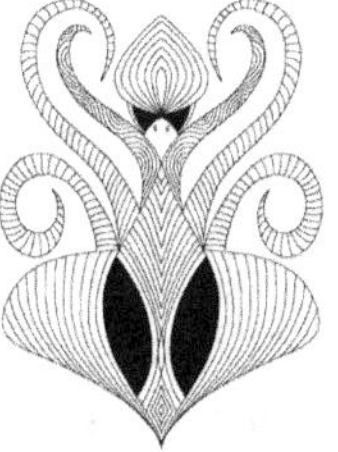
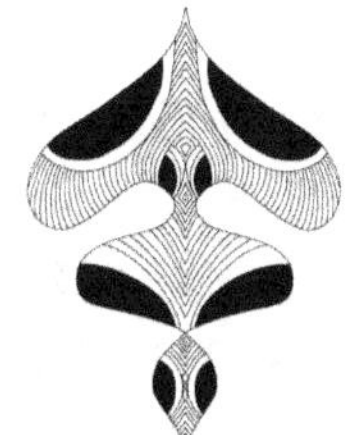
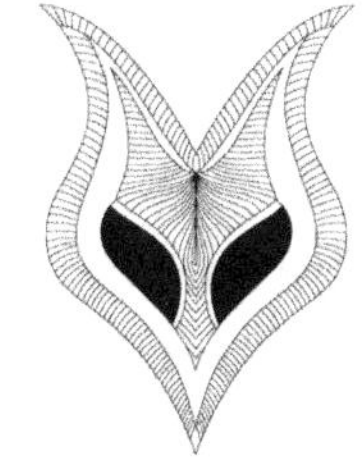
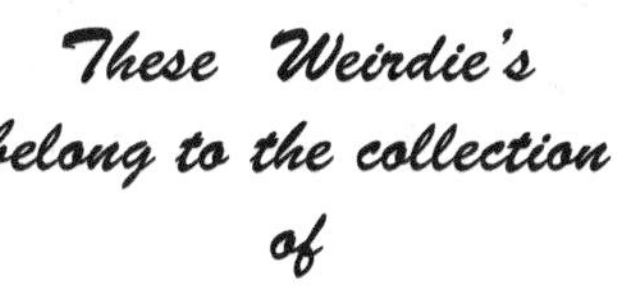
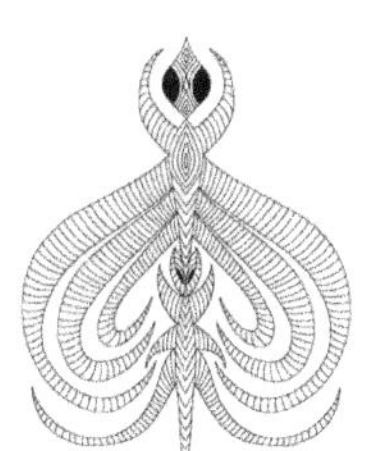

These Weirdie's
belong to the collection
of

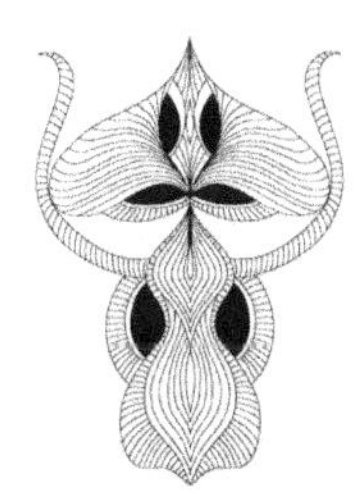
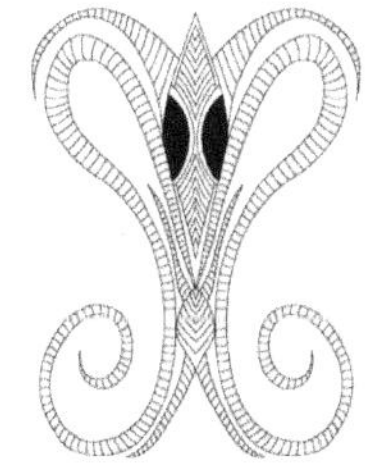
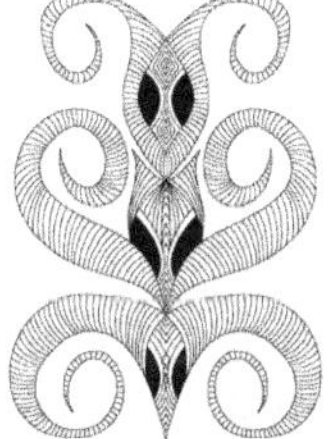
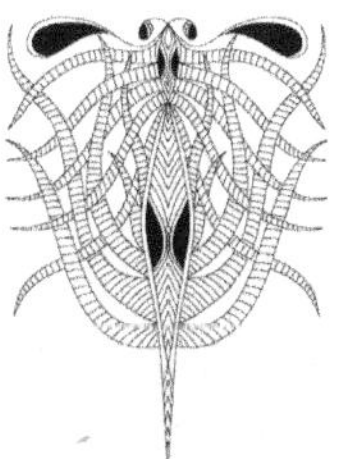
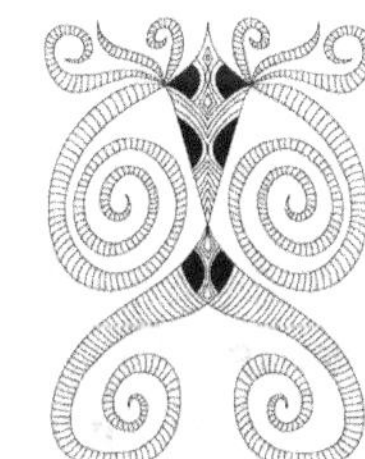
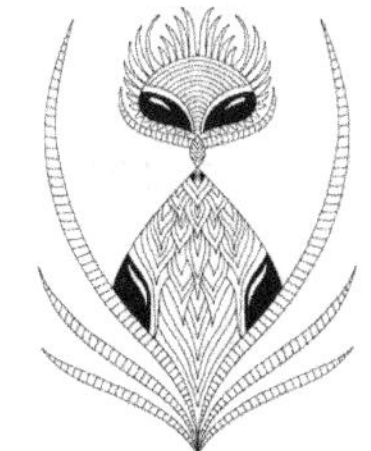
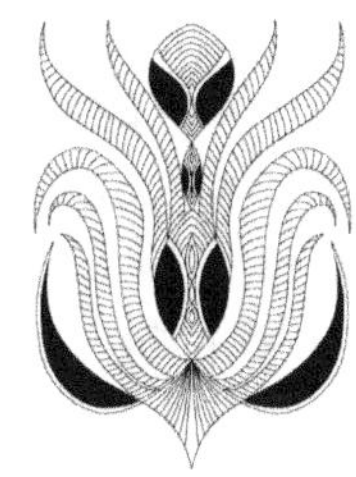
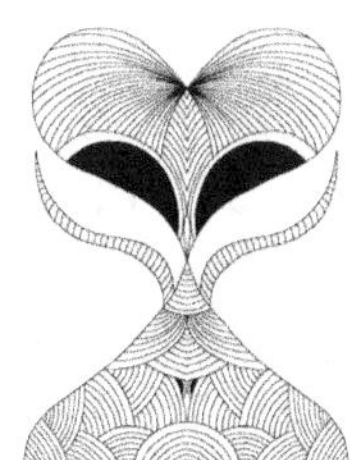
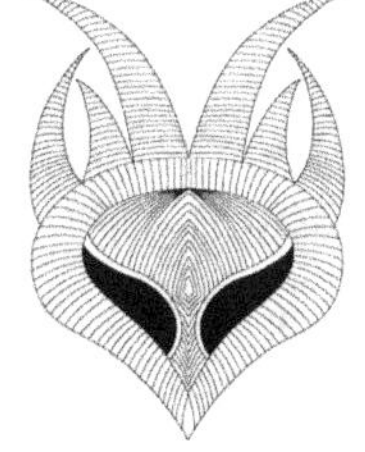
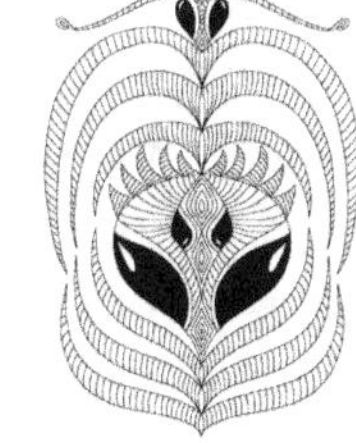
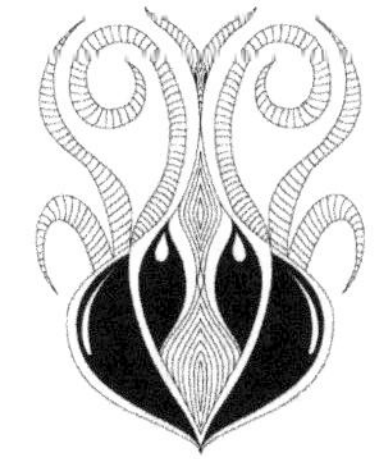
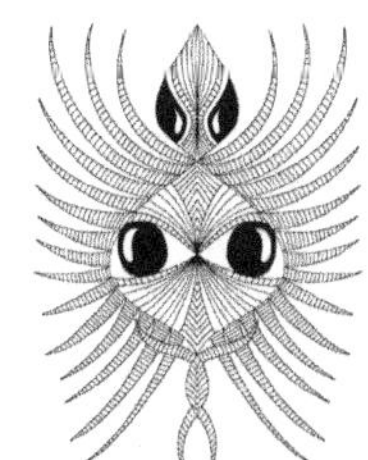
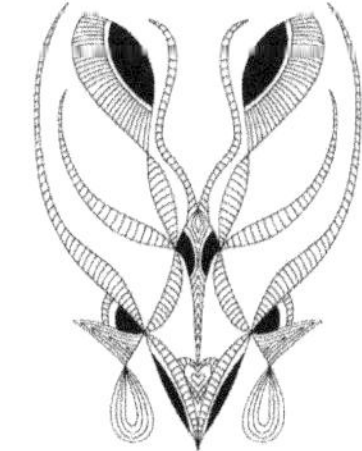
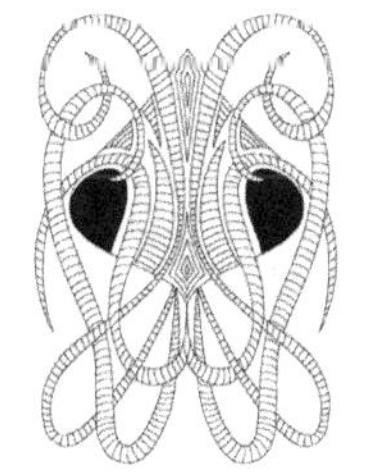
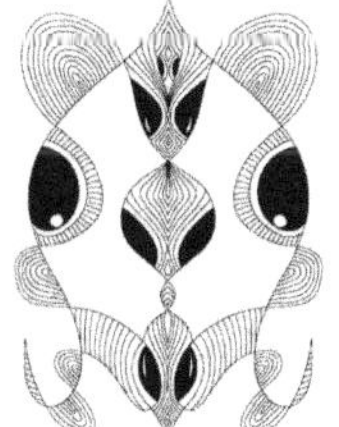

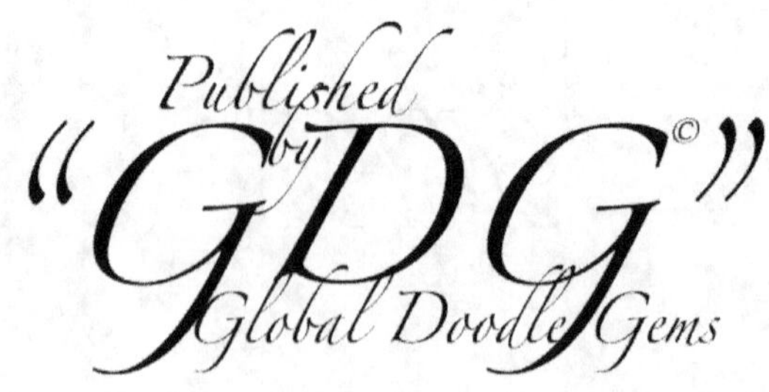

Share your colored versions with us ! We love seeing your results

and hearing from you

we are social !

The Official FB book page, stay on top of what we have in the works !
www.facebook.com/AMVWART
The Community group, share your colored pages, meet the artists, enjoy exclusive freebies, take
part in community Charity books and so much more......
www.facebook.com/groups/ColorAWeirdieADay
Follow us on Twitter.... @GlobalDoodlegem
We are on Instagram too
@globaldoodlegems for instagram
...and if you are not social like that we have a blog
globaldoodlegems.wordpress.com

Welcome to my world of Weirdies

This is the eleventh weirdies book of year 4 of Color A Weirdie A Day,
join us for daily coloring with either me or one of the wonderful guesthosts
at the group www.facebook.com/groups/ColorAWeirdieADay,
and check out all the beautiful colored !
The set has 12 books Weirdies 37 to Weirdies 48, one book for each month
with a Weirdie for each day, additionally all Weirdies are repeated in the
back of the book in their upside_down versions ...
Your Weirdie can drastically change and turn in to a brand new Weirdie.
Get your Weirdie on and have a fun and relaxing time with coloring it,
join the group and show your colored, join the live coloring and have fun
with us ... if you like !
Weirdies 1 to 12 were colored live in 2018 Weirdies 13 to 24 were colo-
red live in 2019 Weirdies 25 to 36 were colored 2020

Weirdies 37 will be colored in January 2021 Daily
Weirdies 38 will be colored in February 2021 Daily
Weirdies 39 will be colored in March 2021 Daily
Weirdies 40 will be colored in April 2021 Daily
Weirdies 41 will be colored in May 2021 Daily
Weirdies 42 will be colored in June 2021 Daily
Weirdies 43 will be colored in July 2021 Daily
Weirdies 44 will be colored in August 2021 Daily
Weirdies 45 will be colored in September 2021 Daily
Weirdies 46 will be colored in October 2021 Daily
Weirdies 47 will be colored in November 2021 Daily

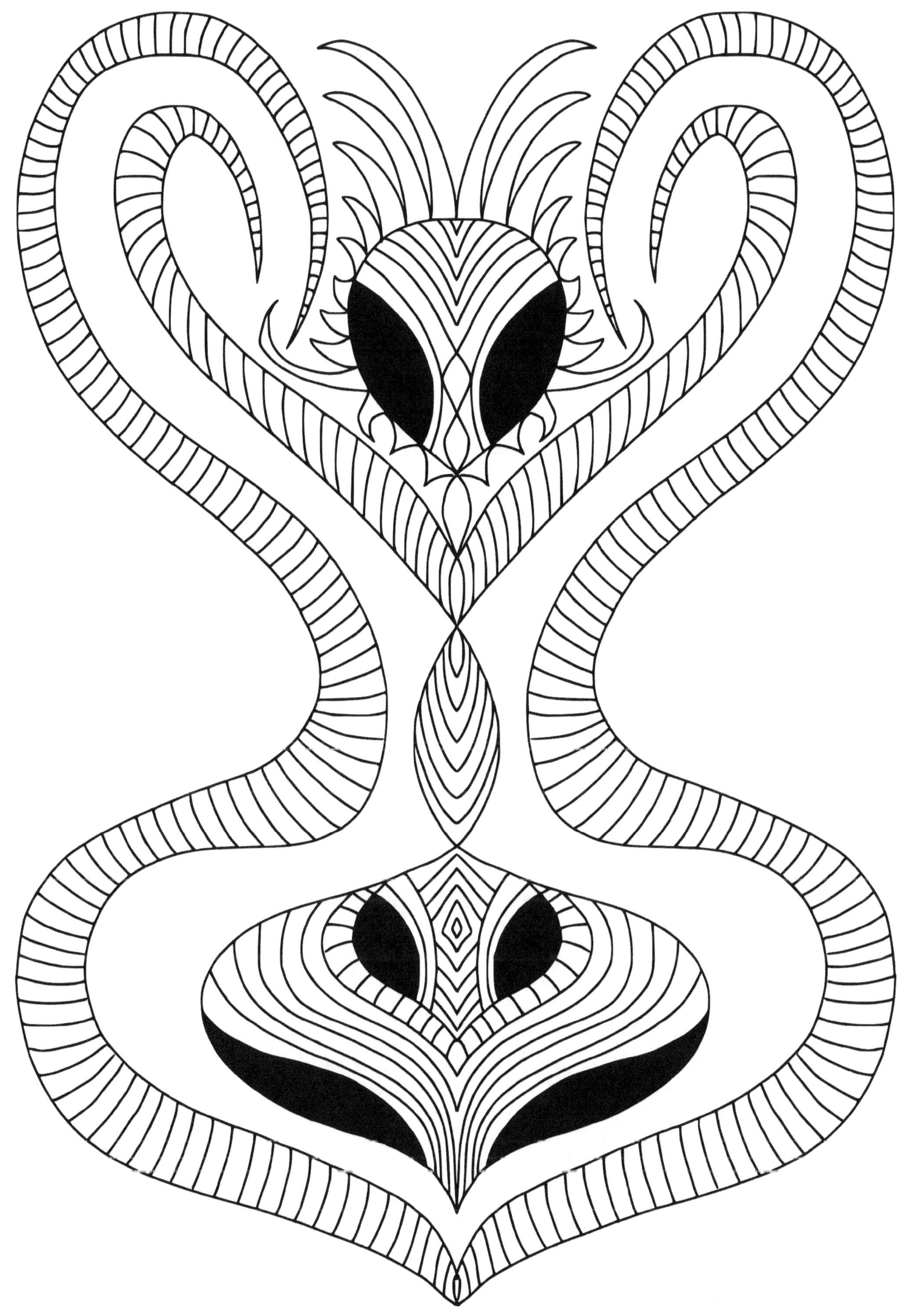

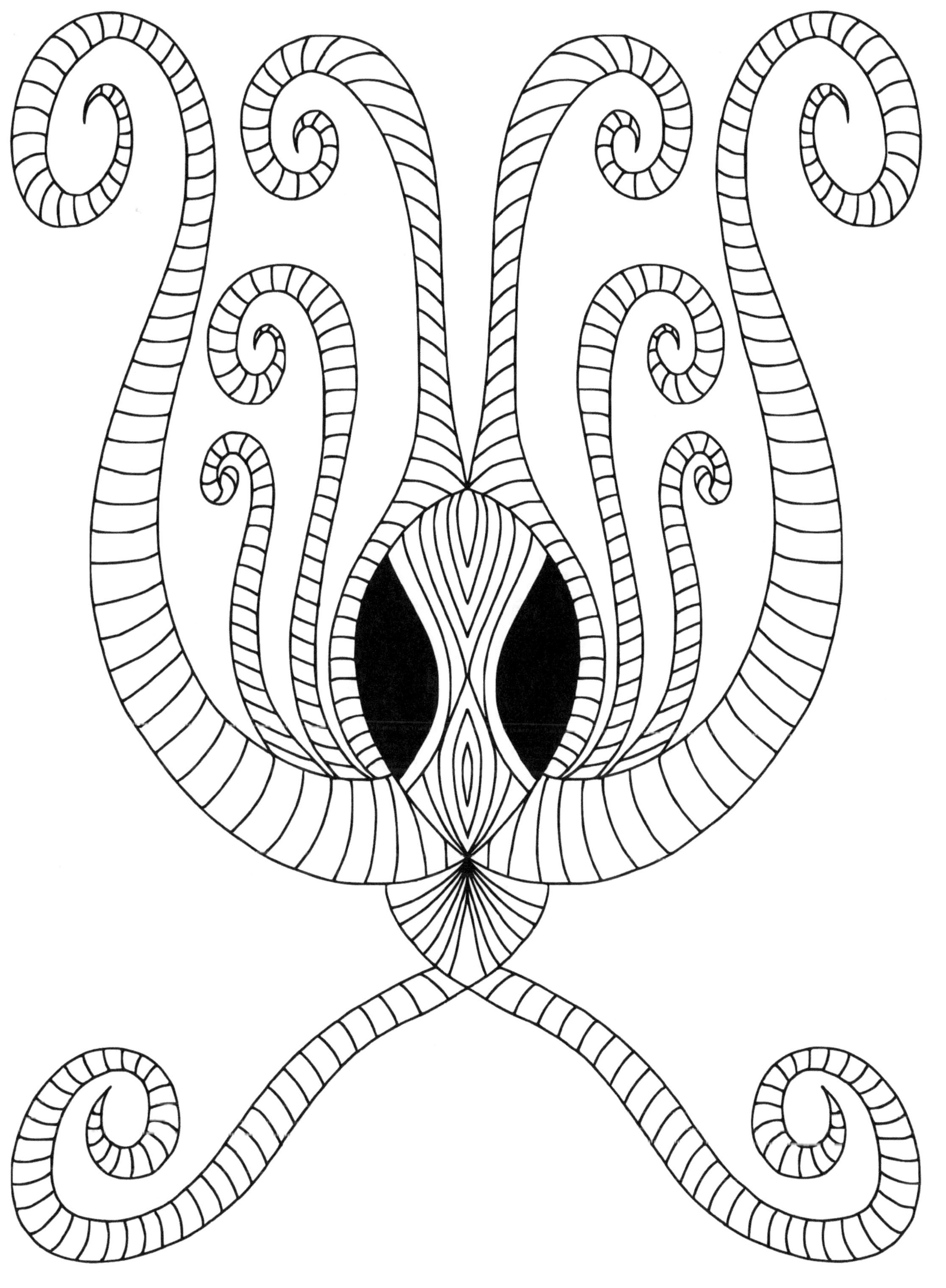

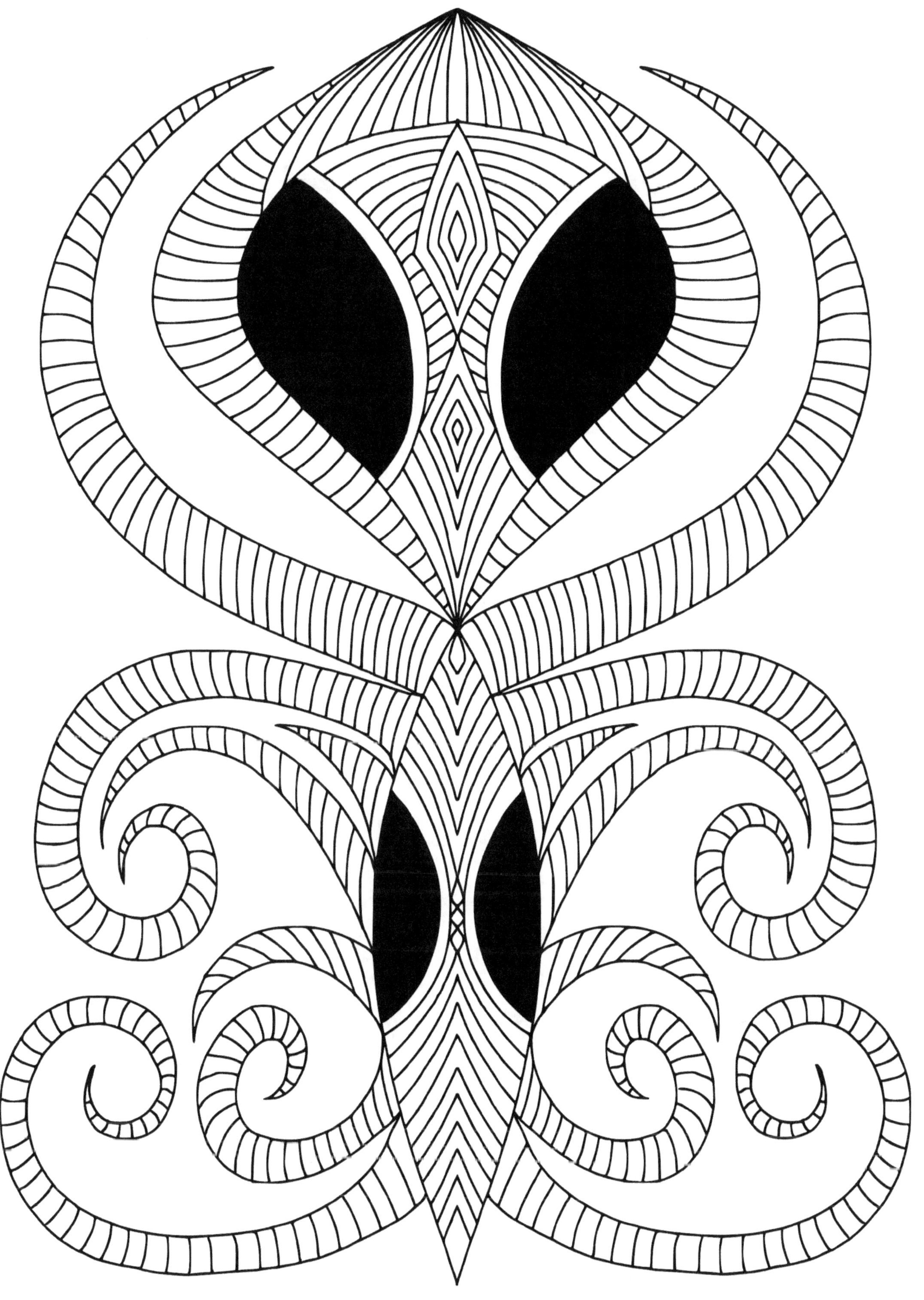

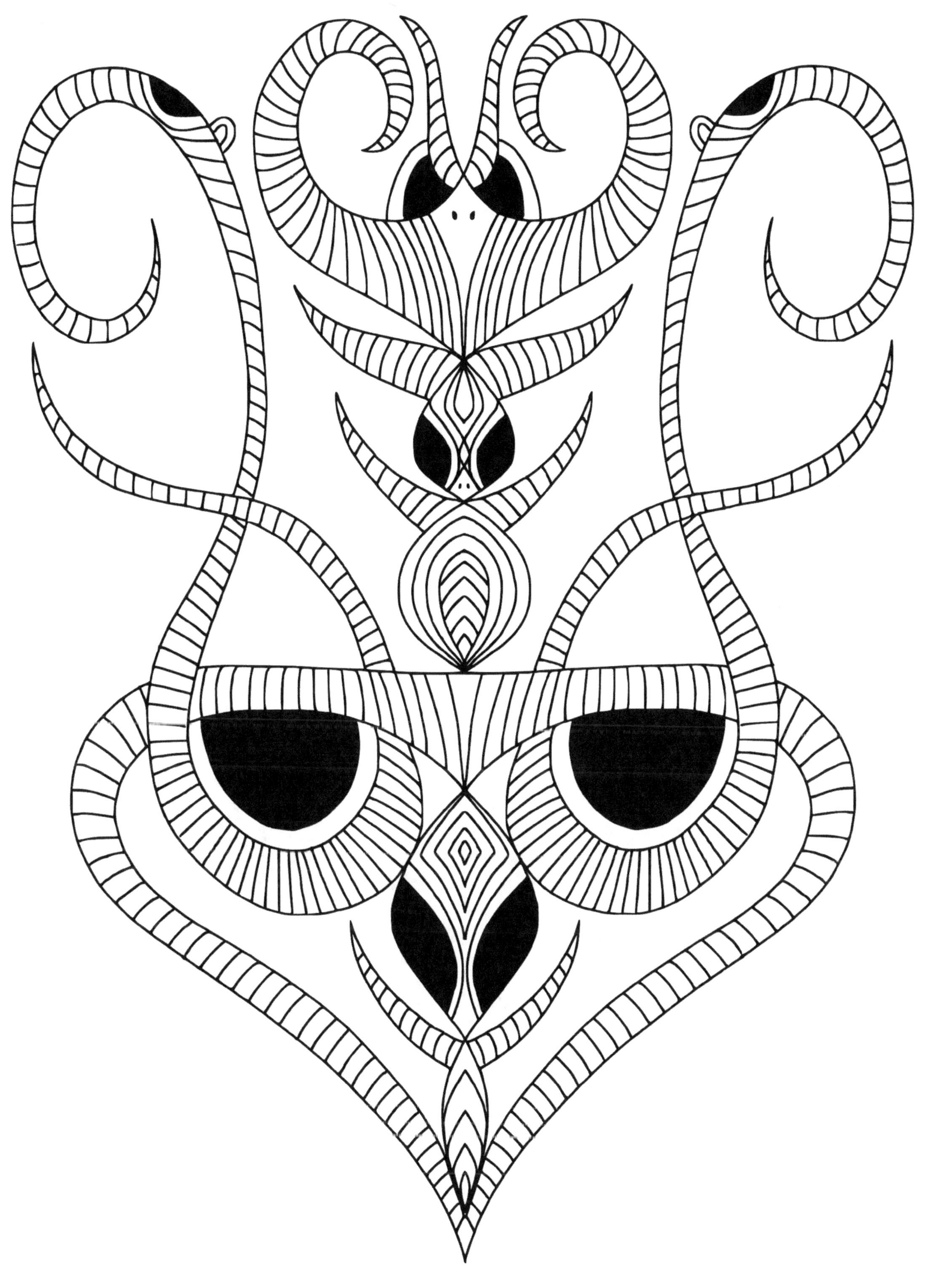

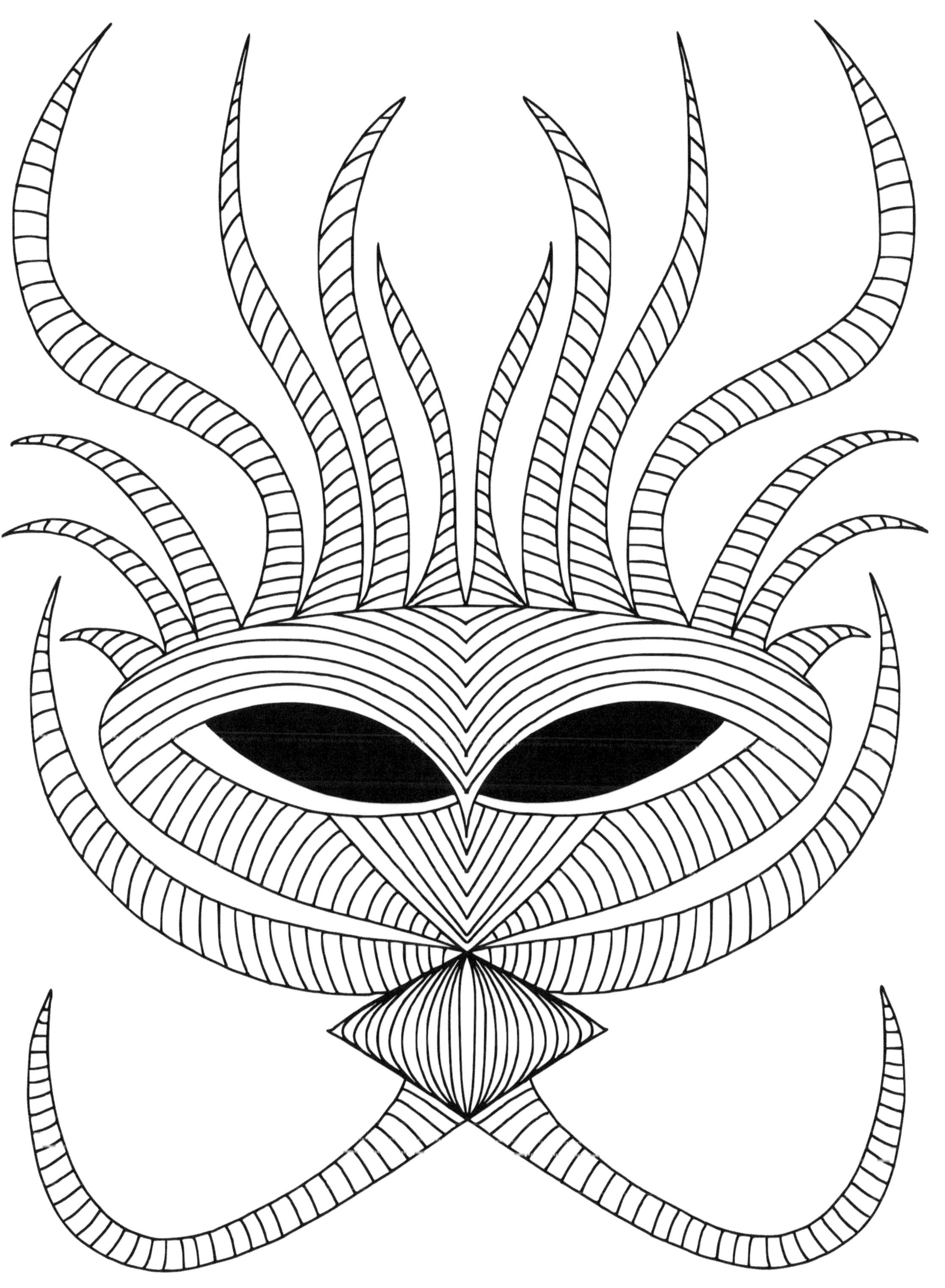

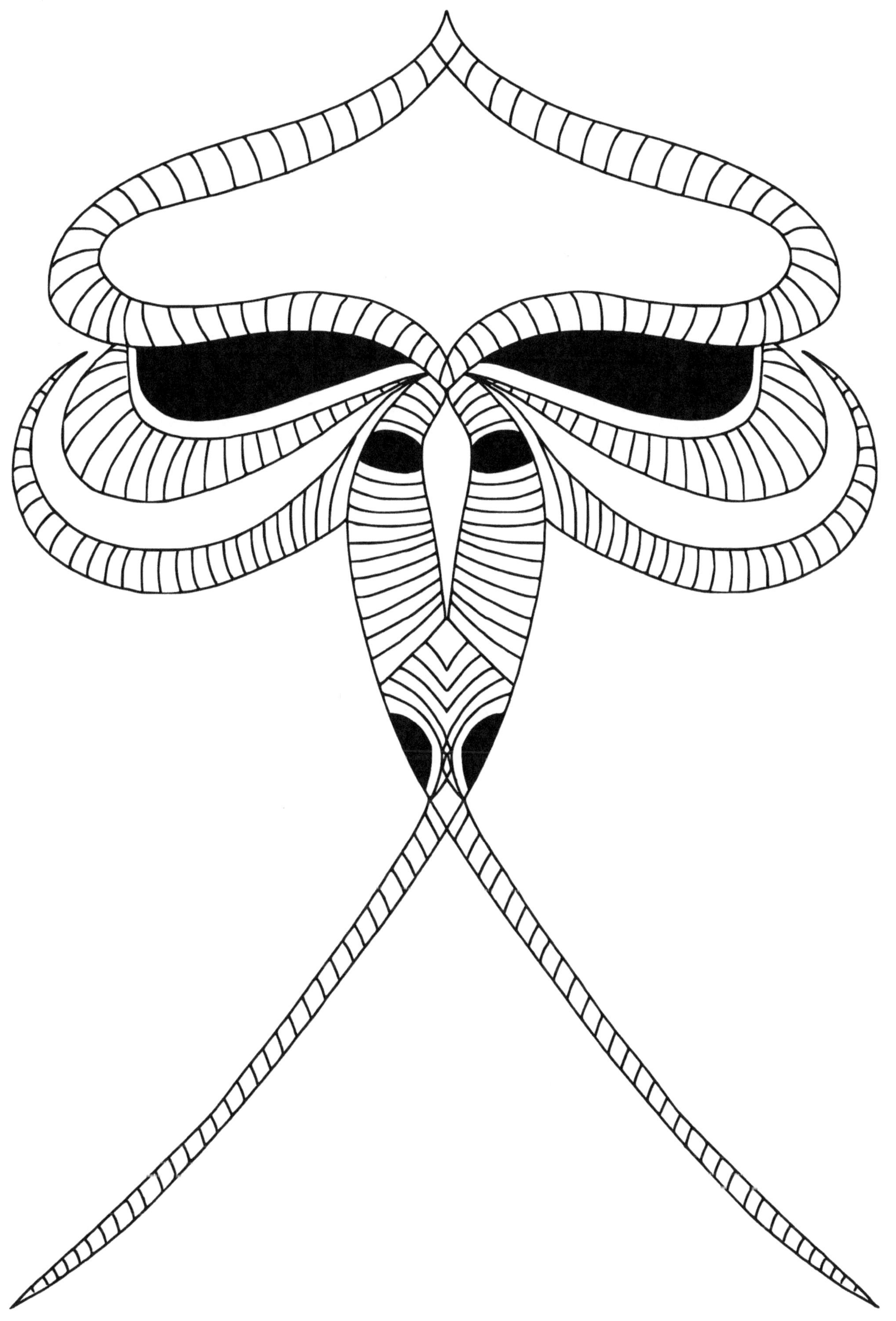

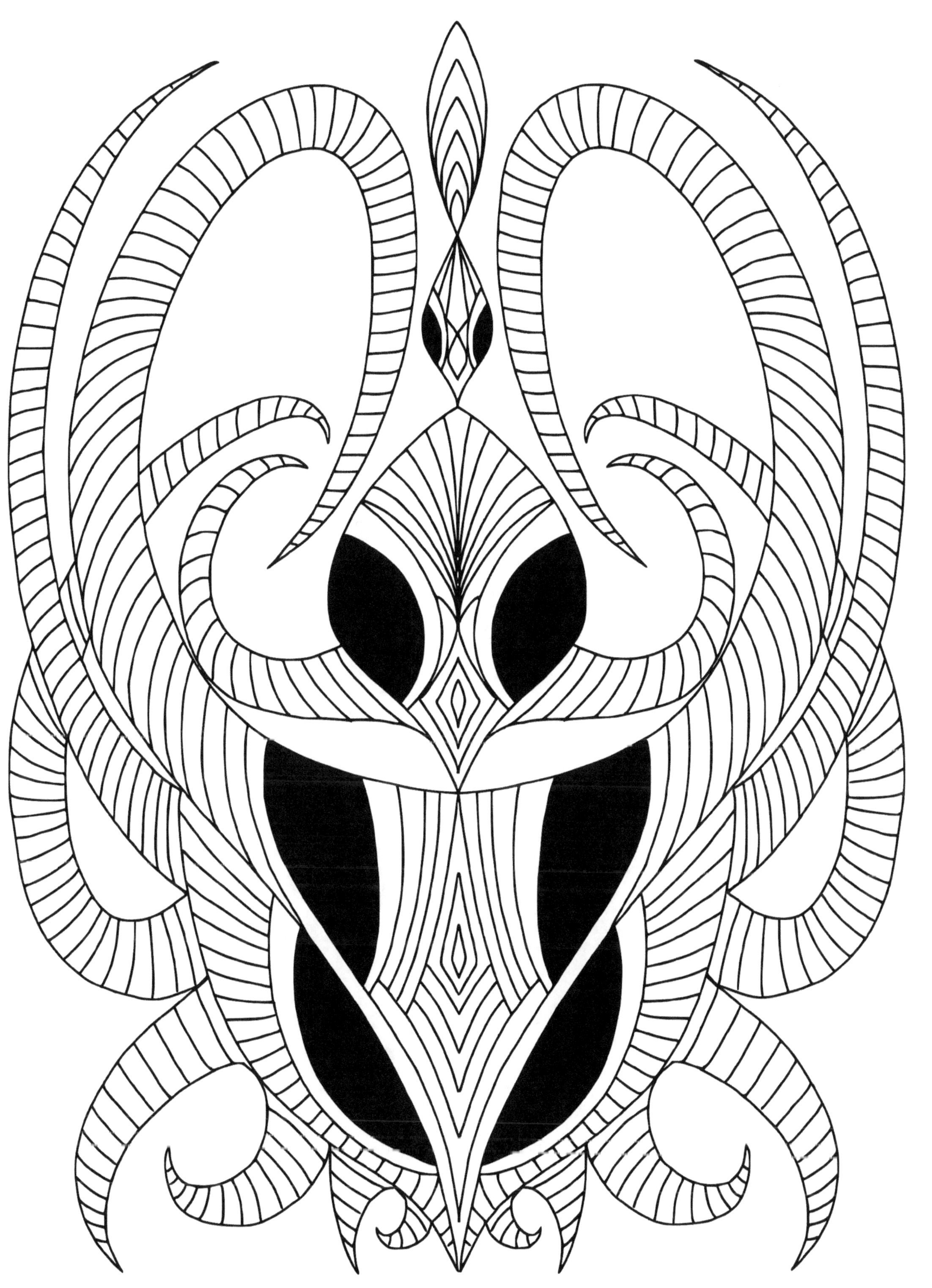

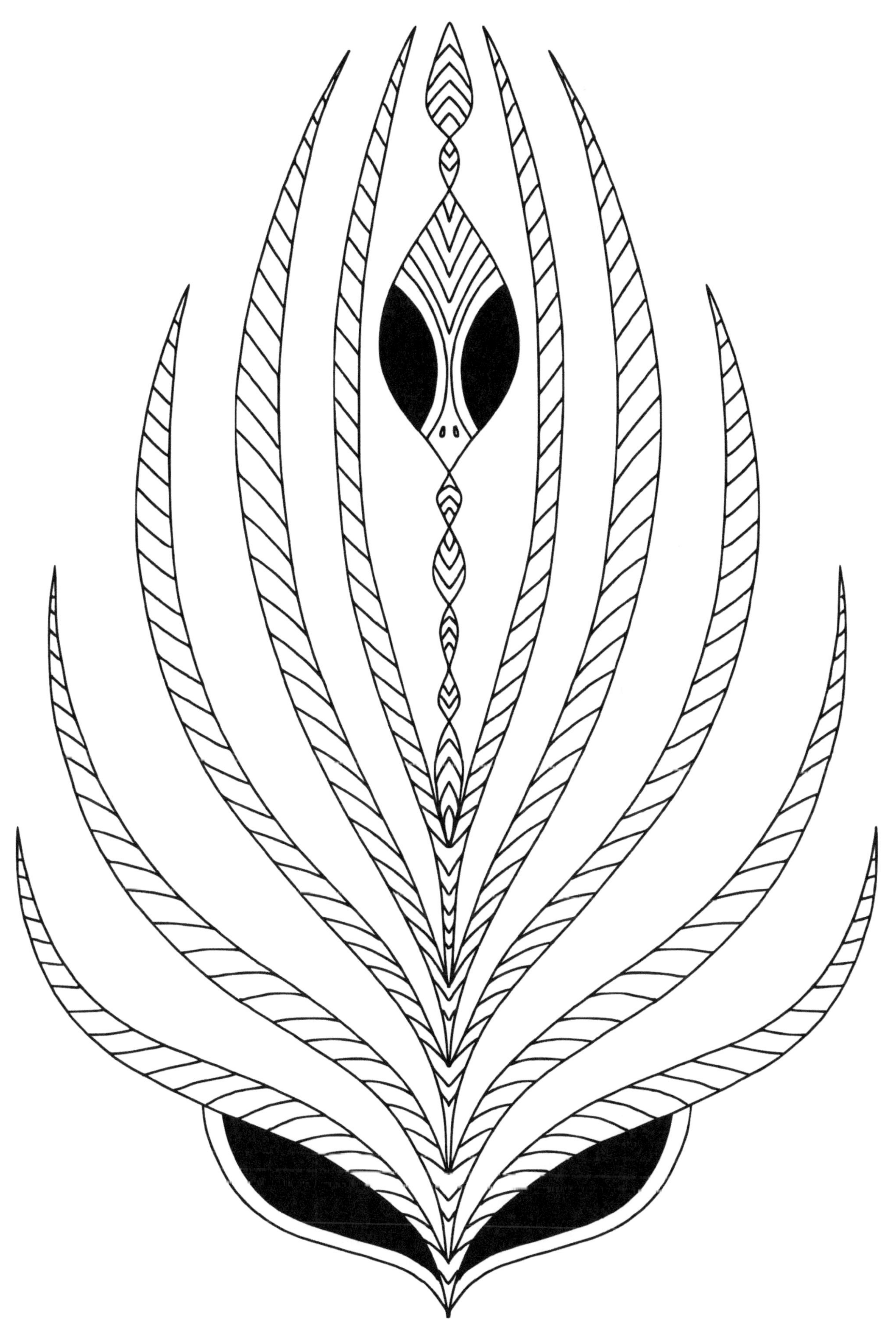

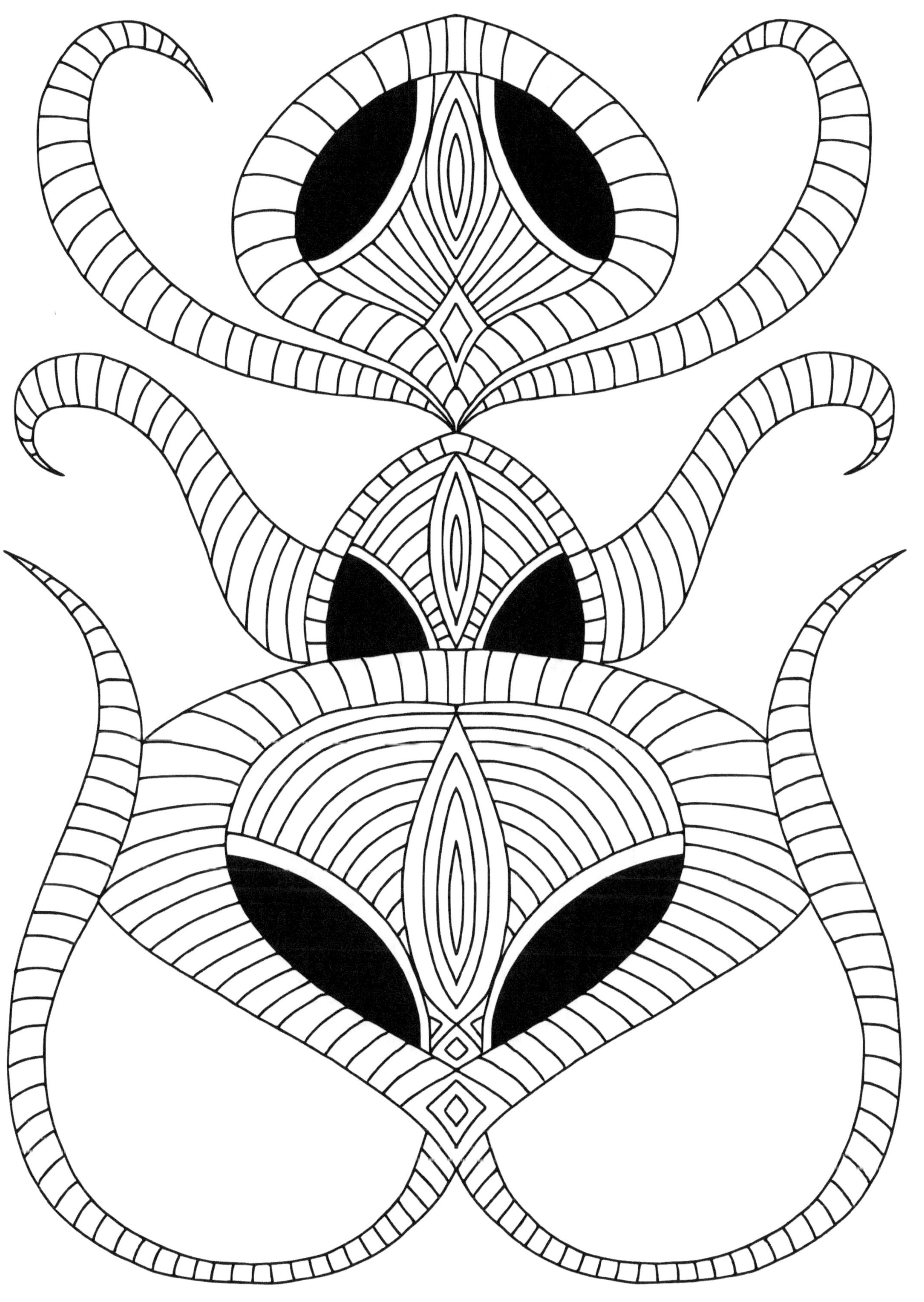

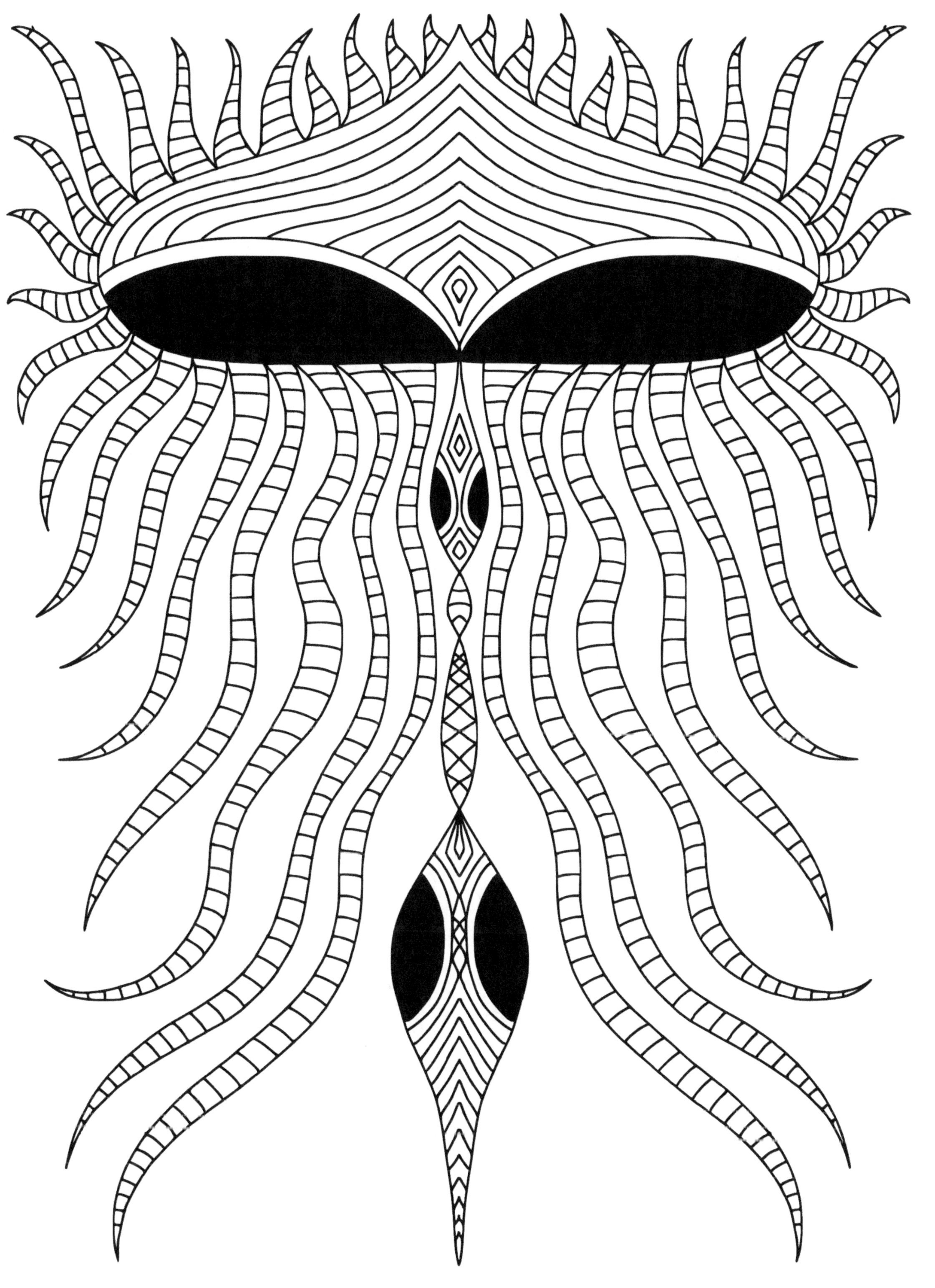

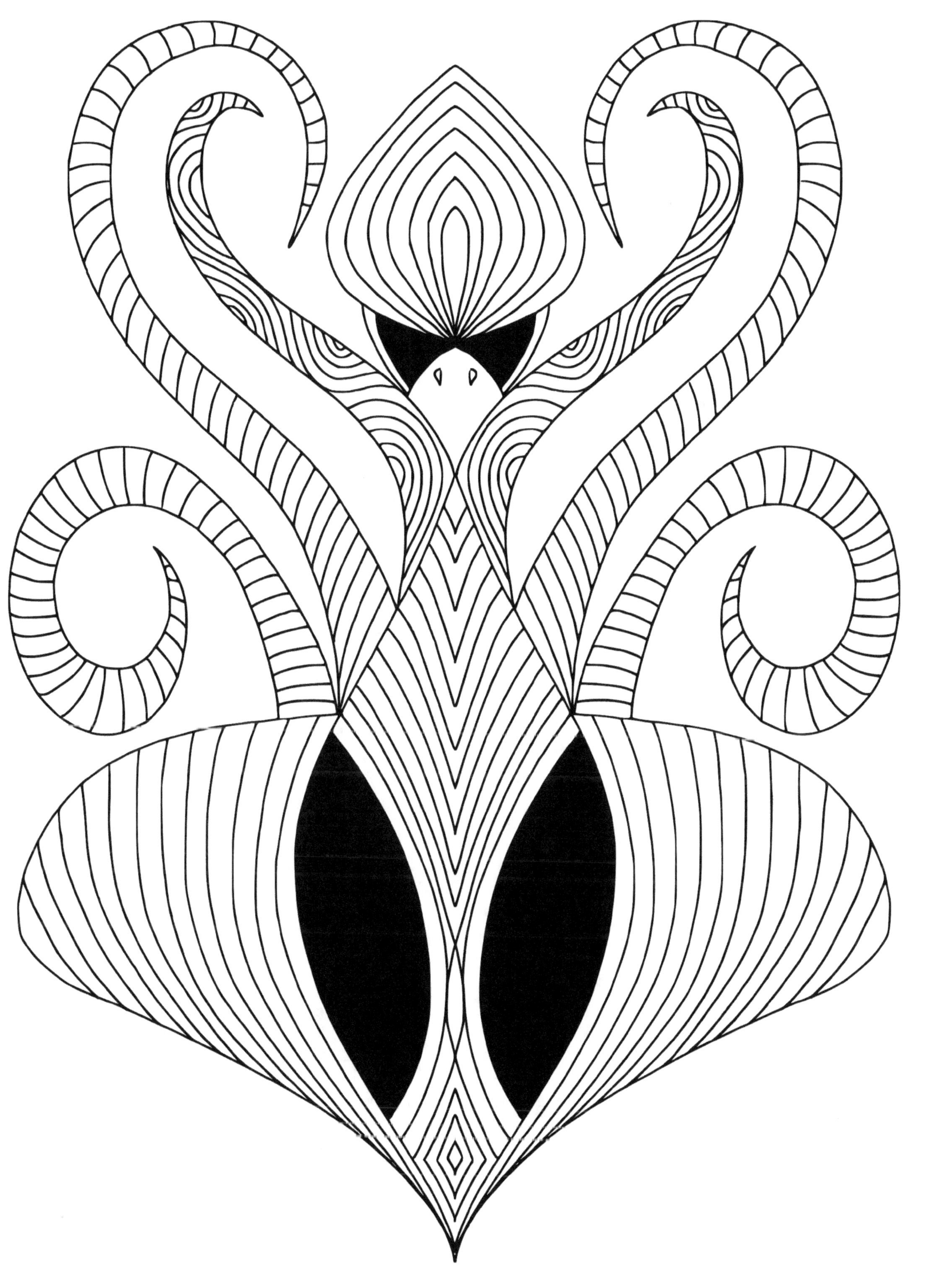

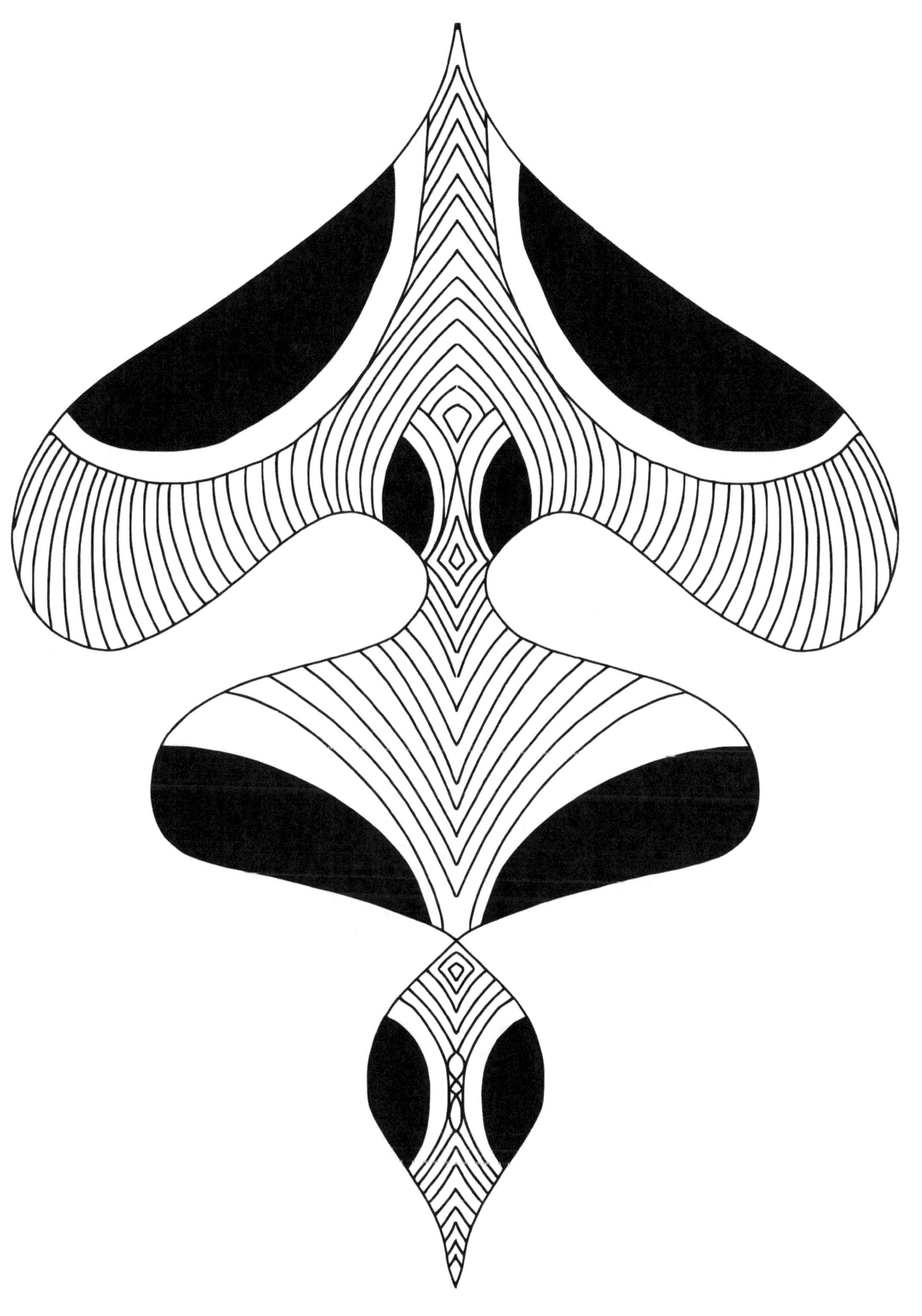

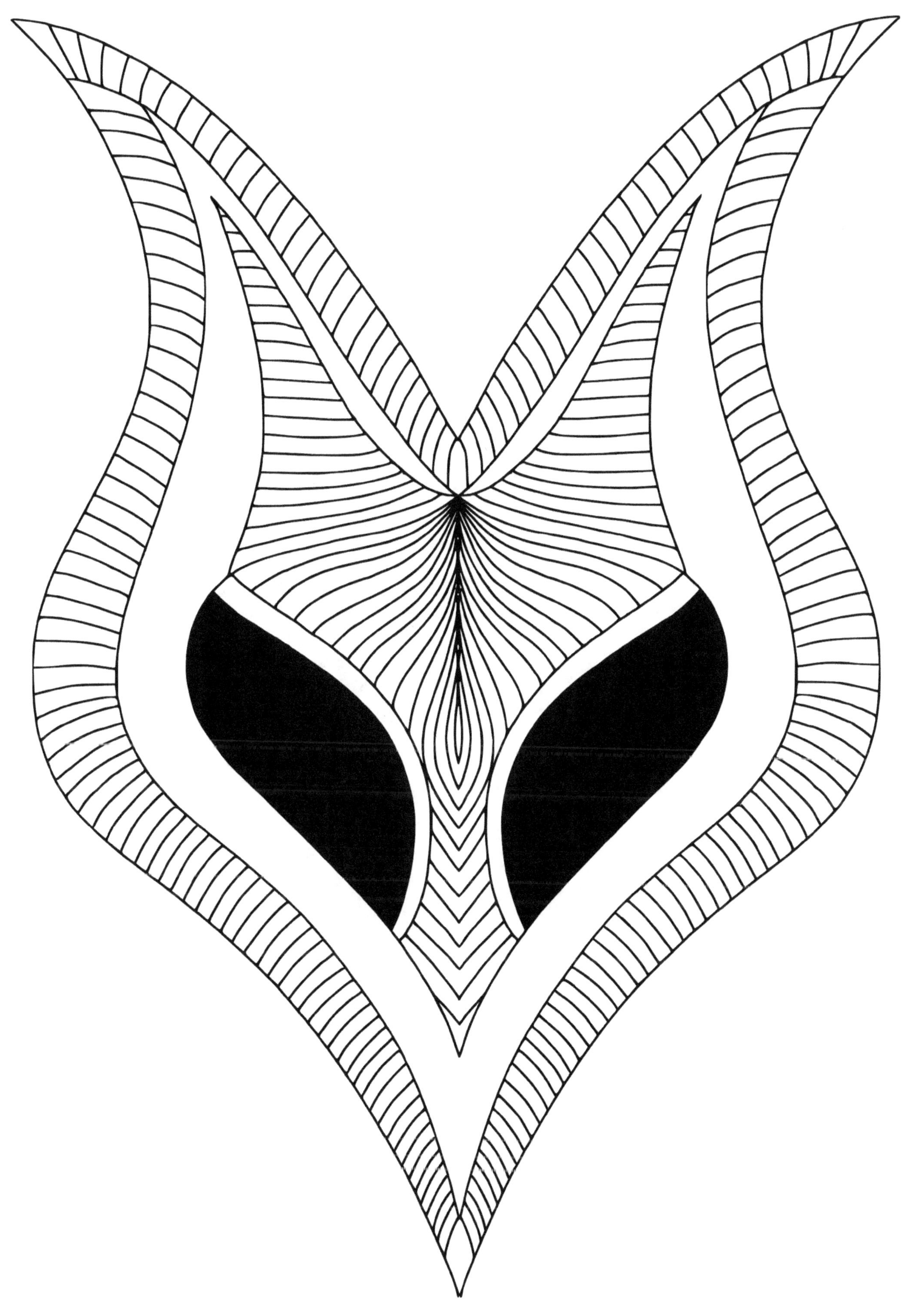

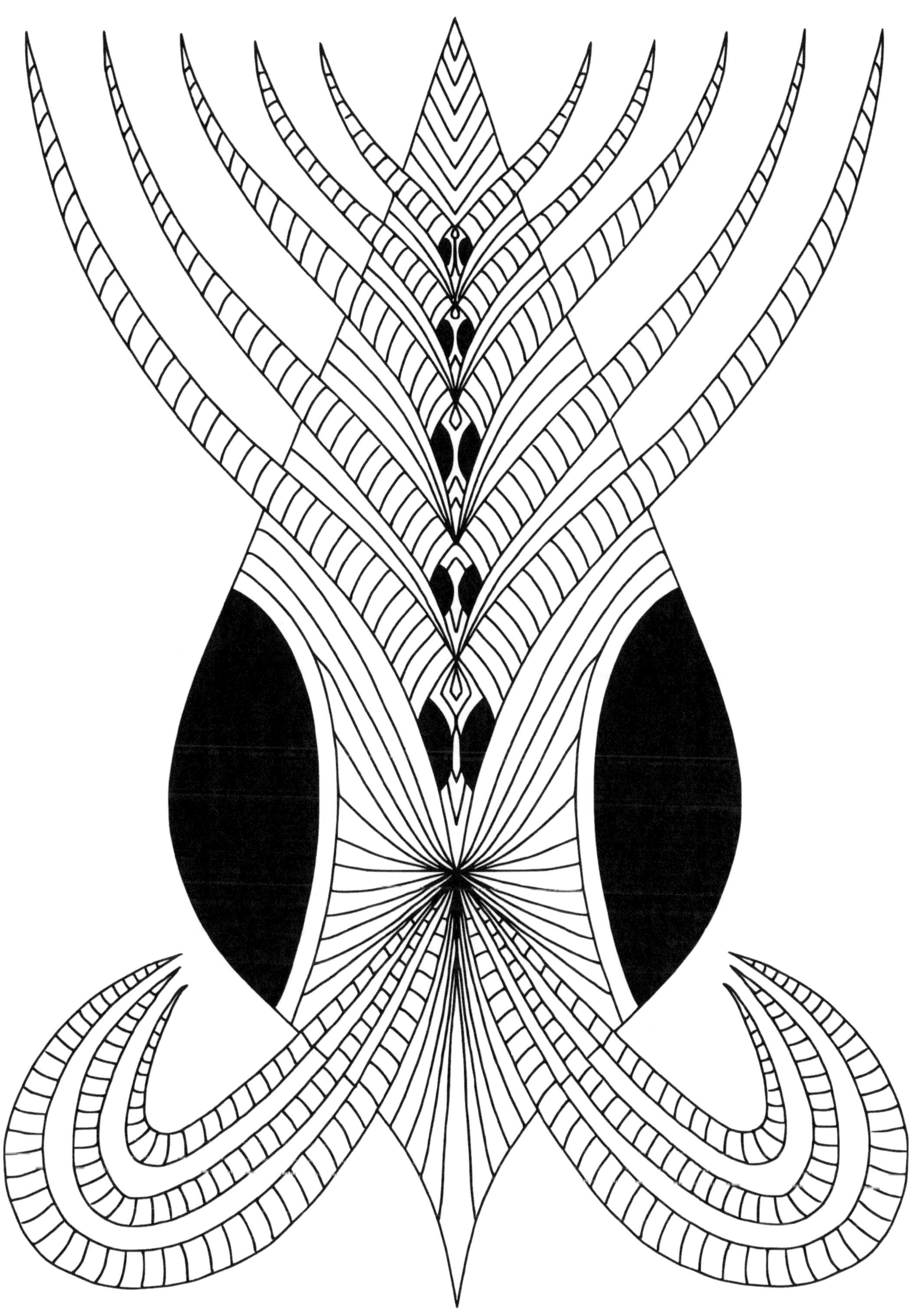

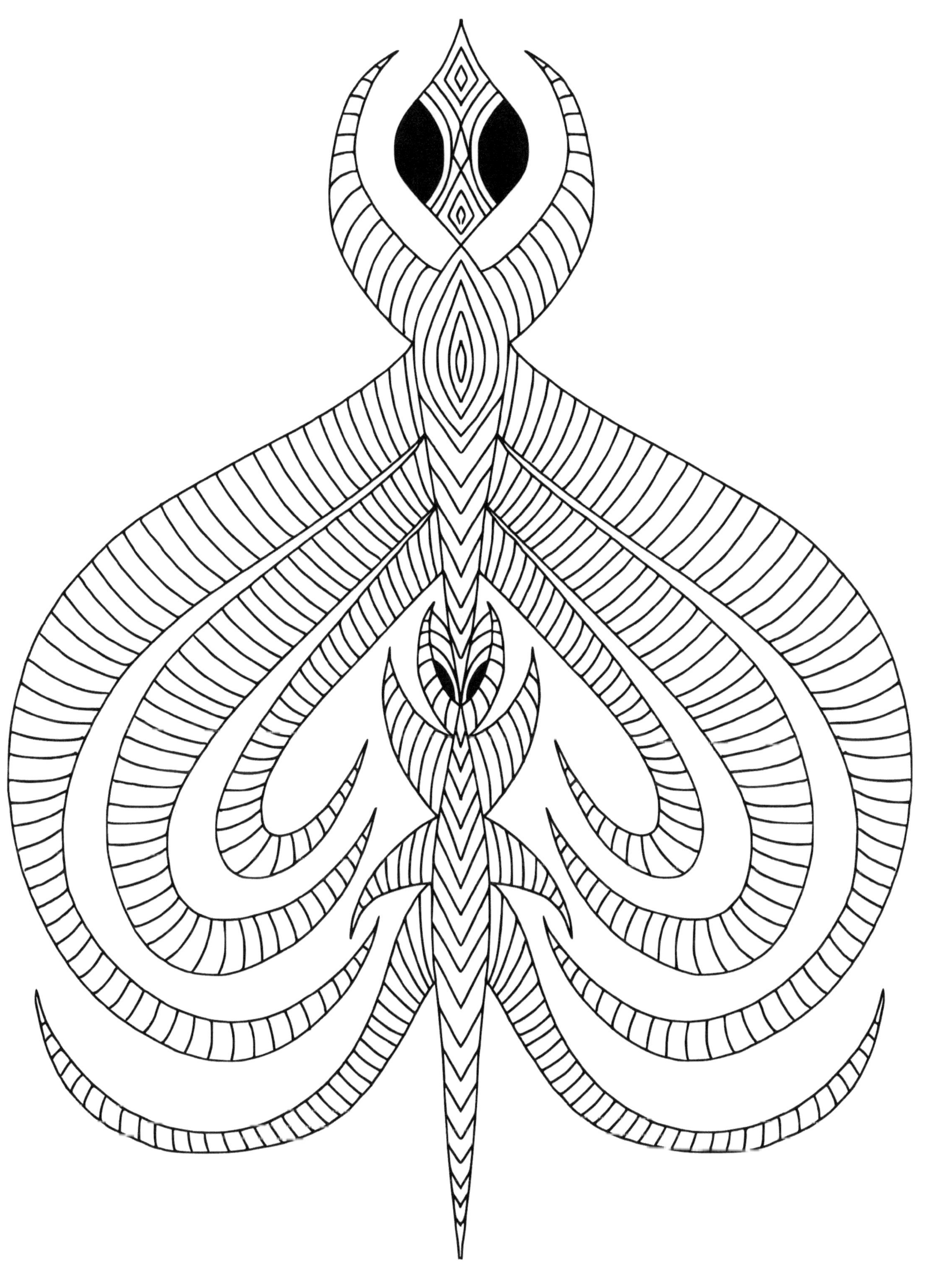

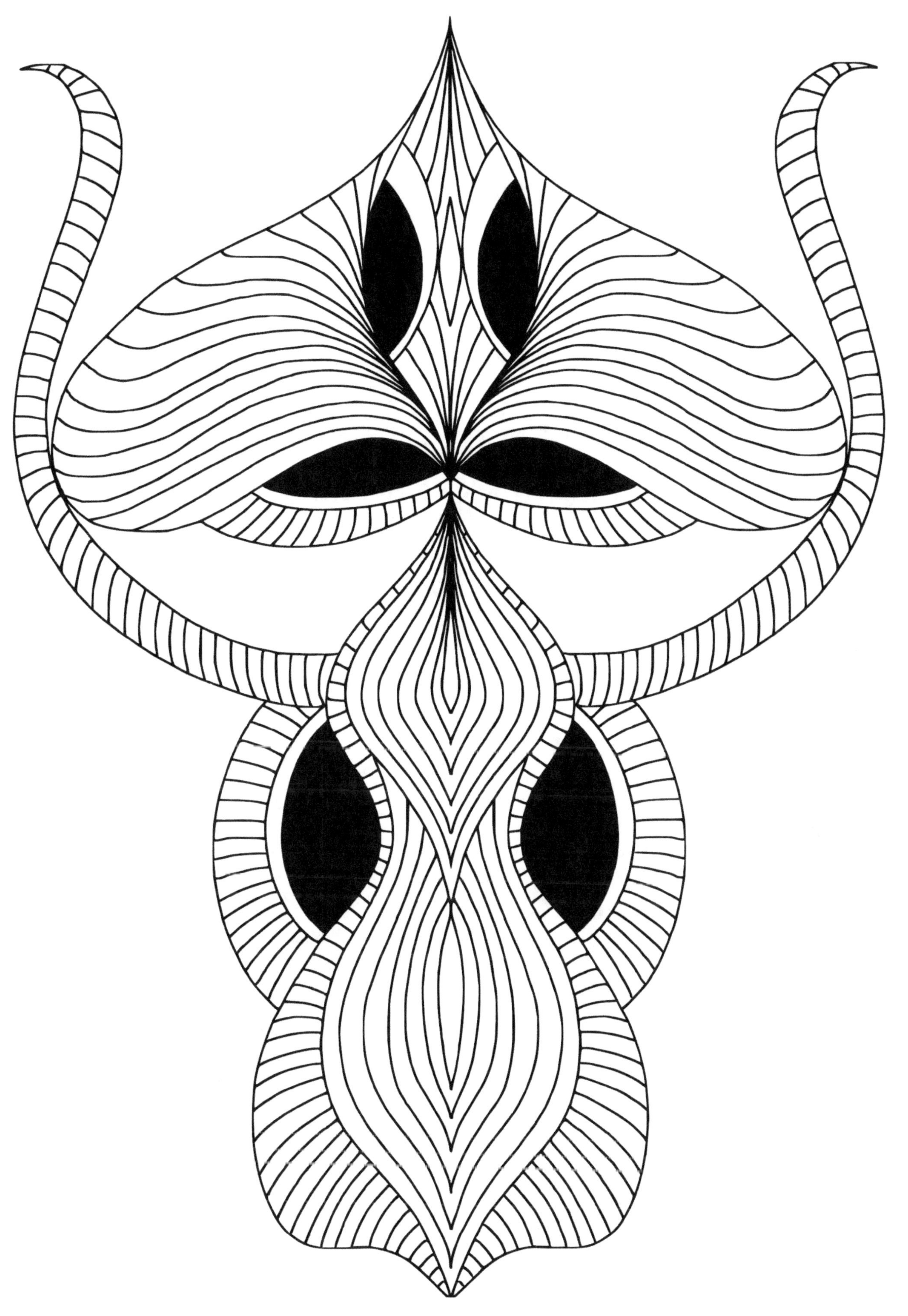

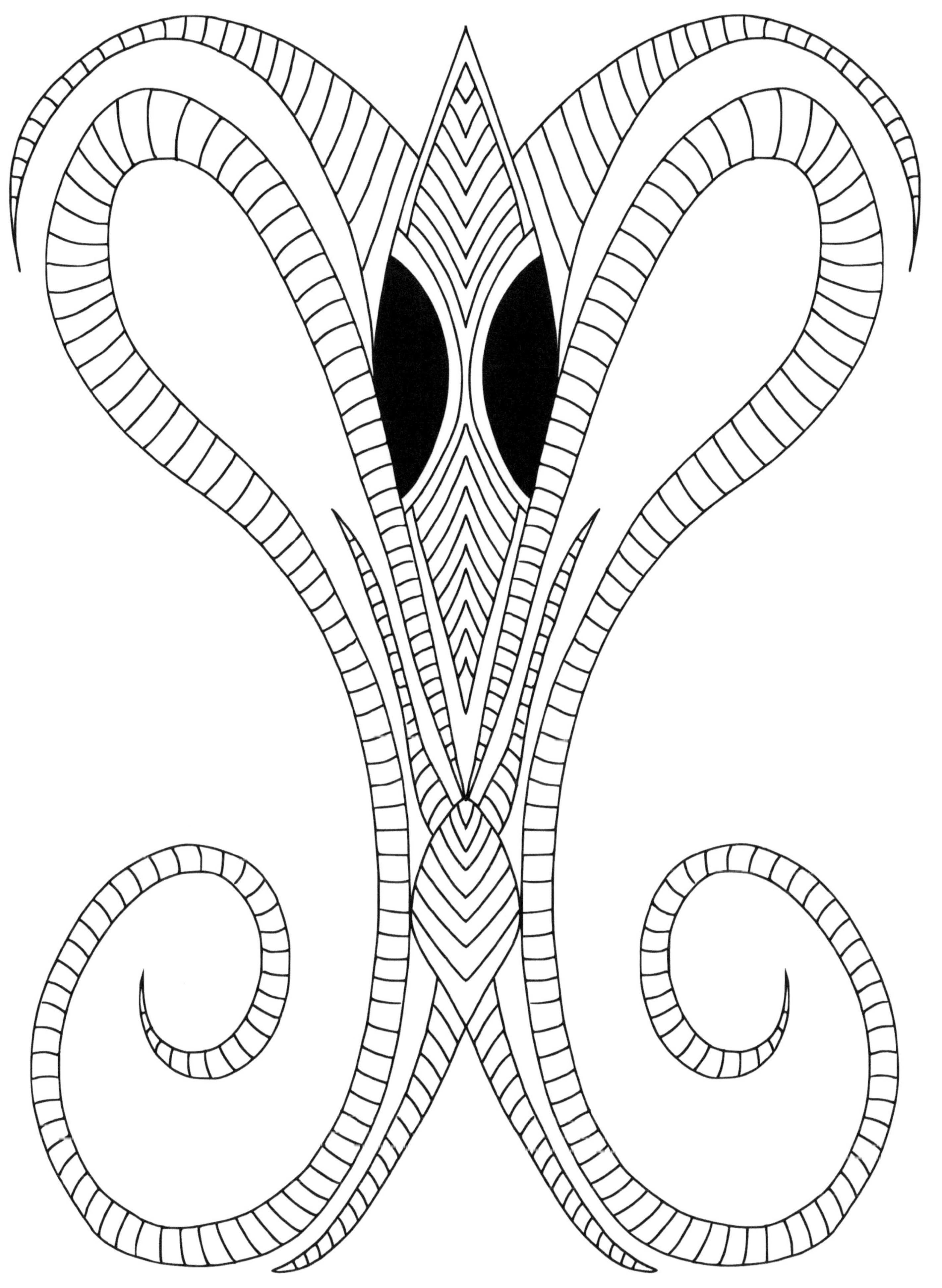

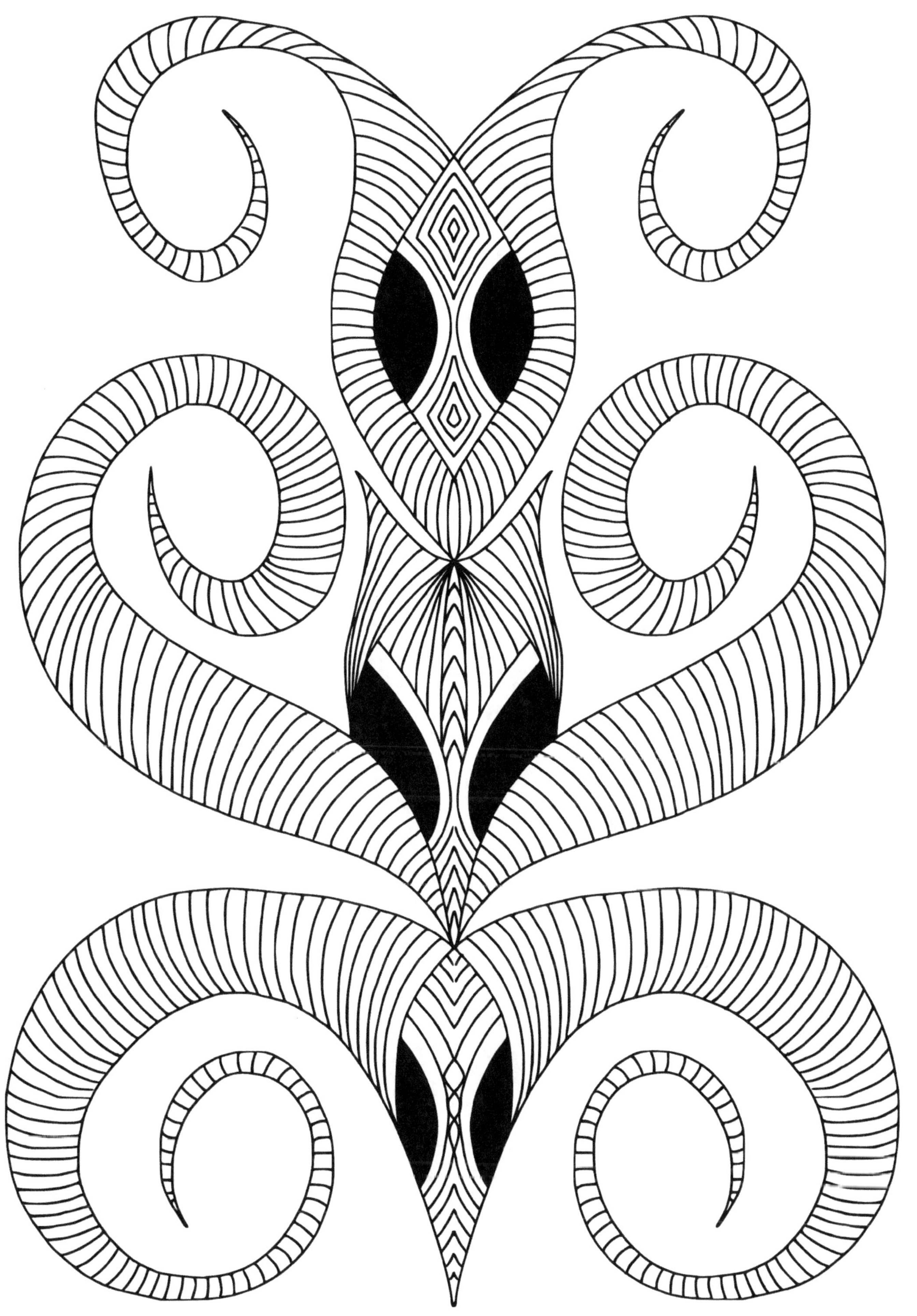

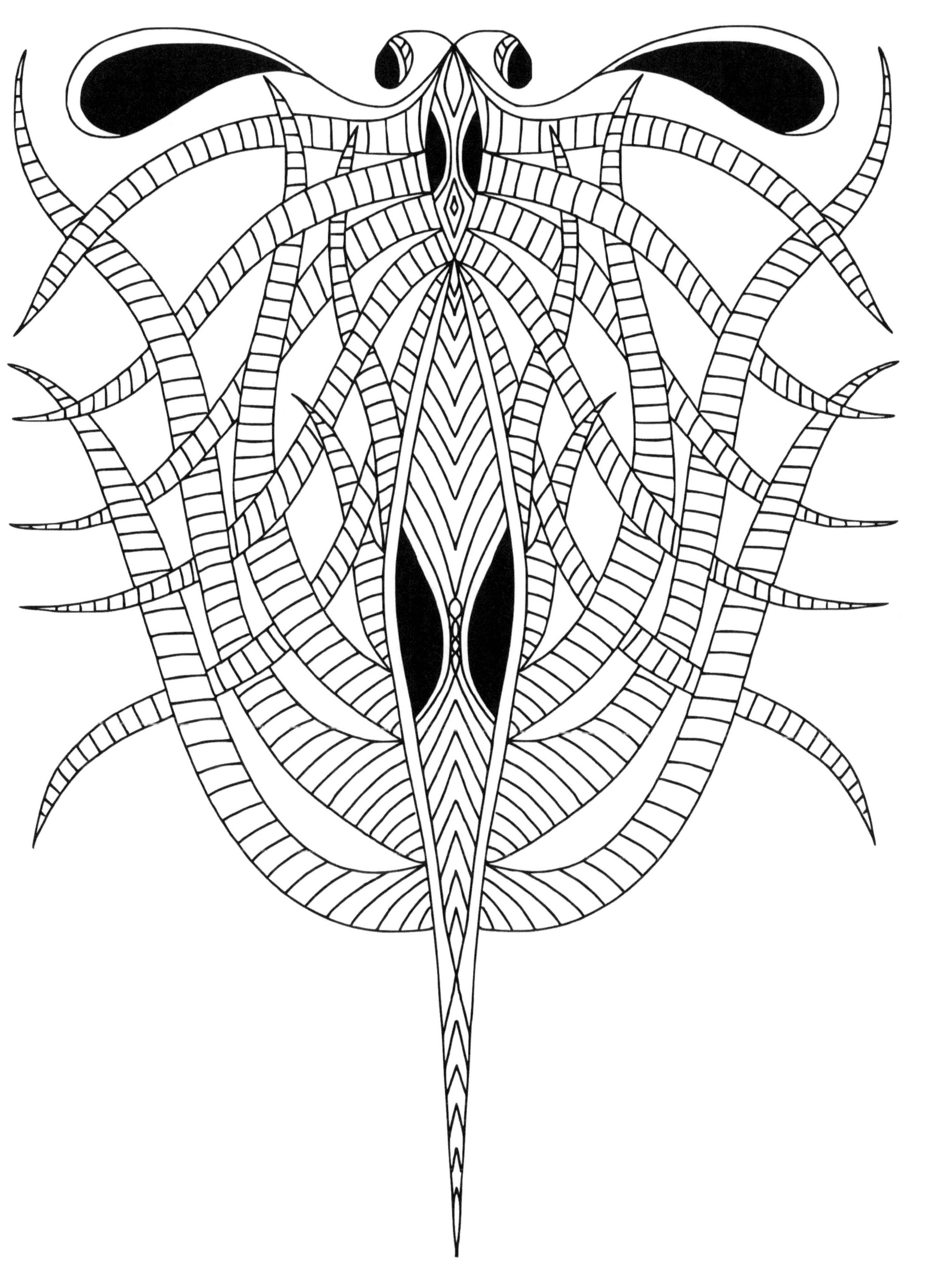

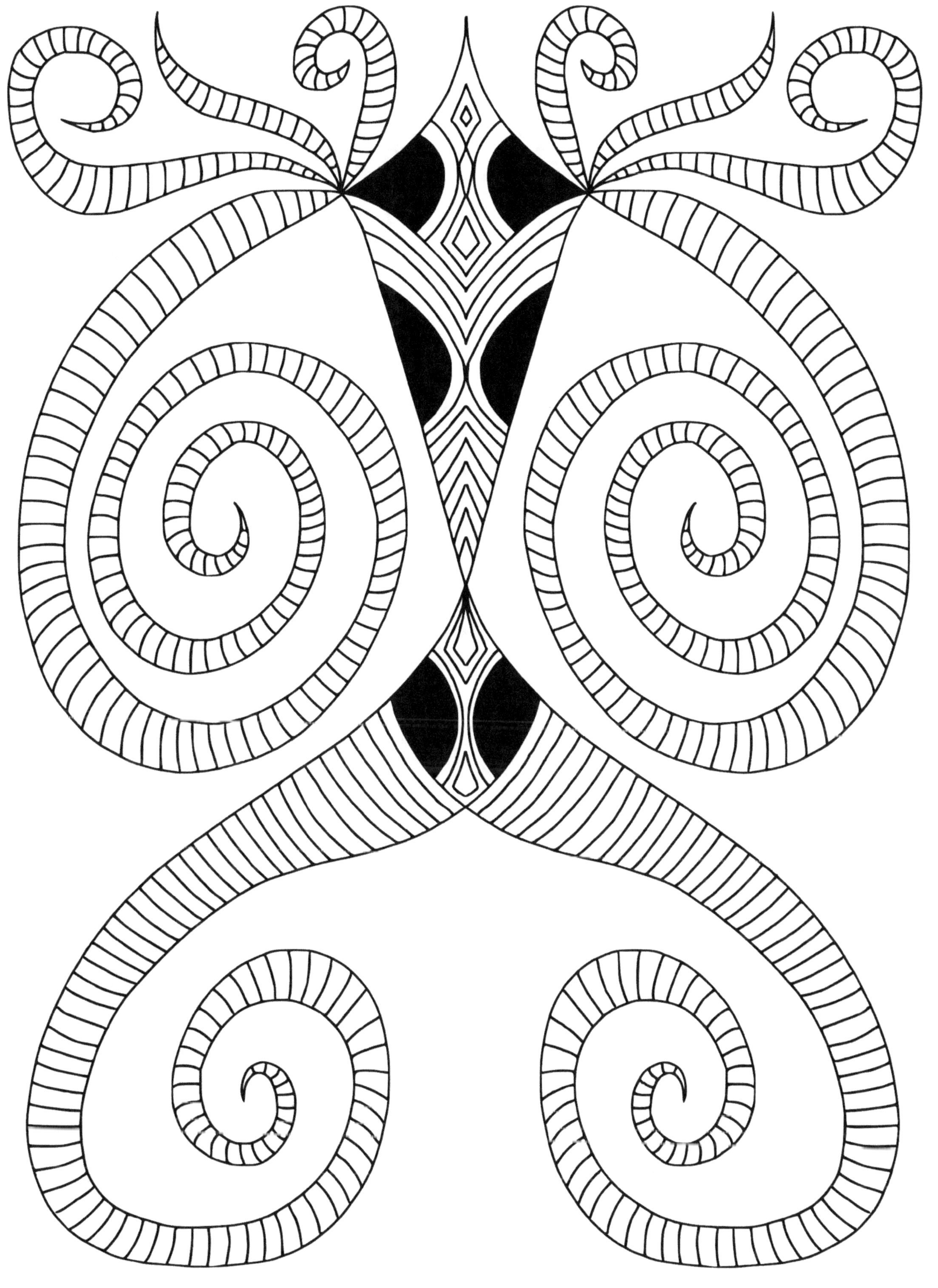

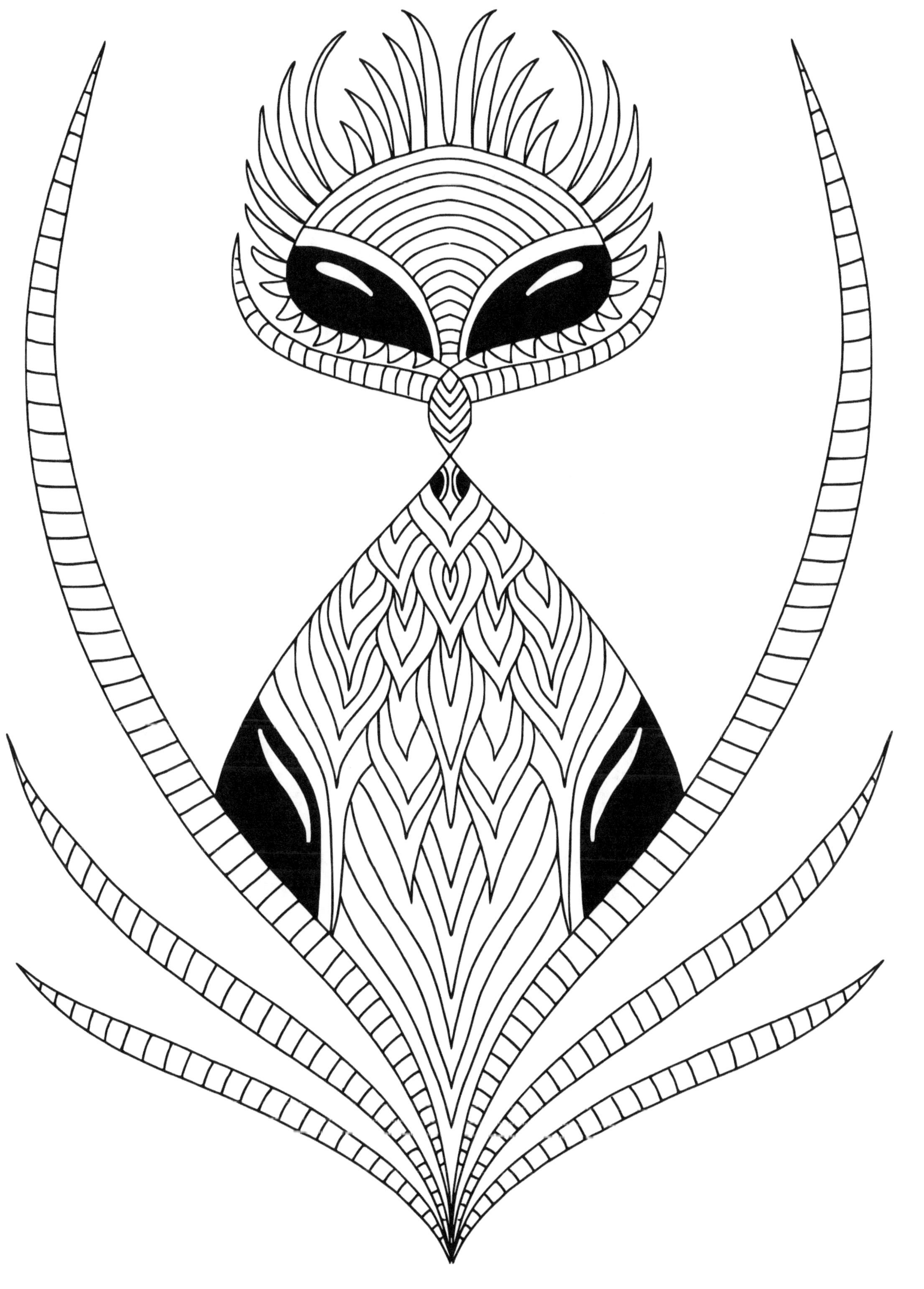

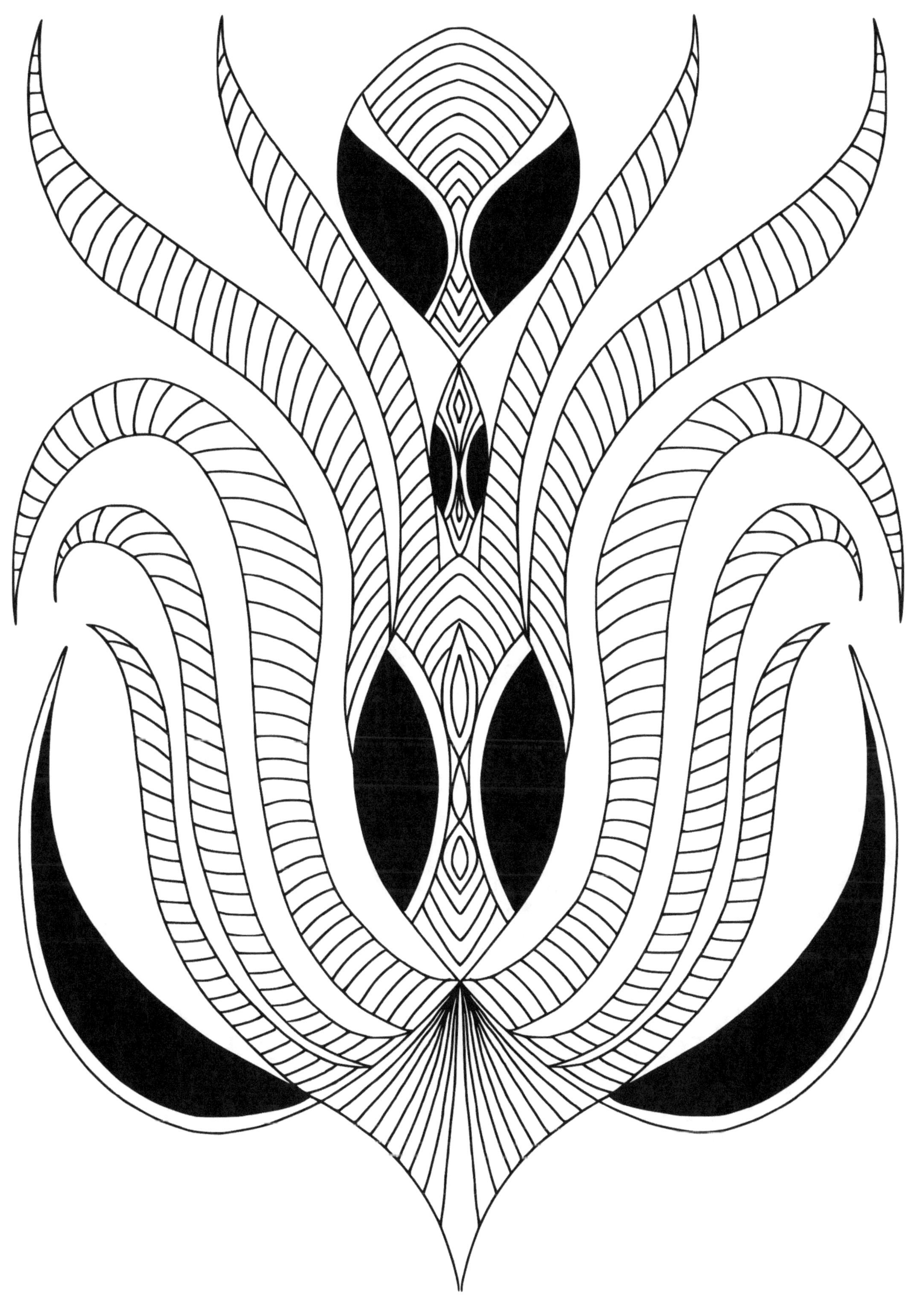

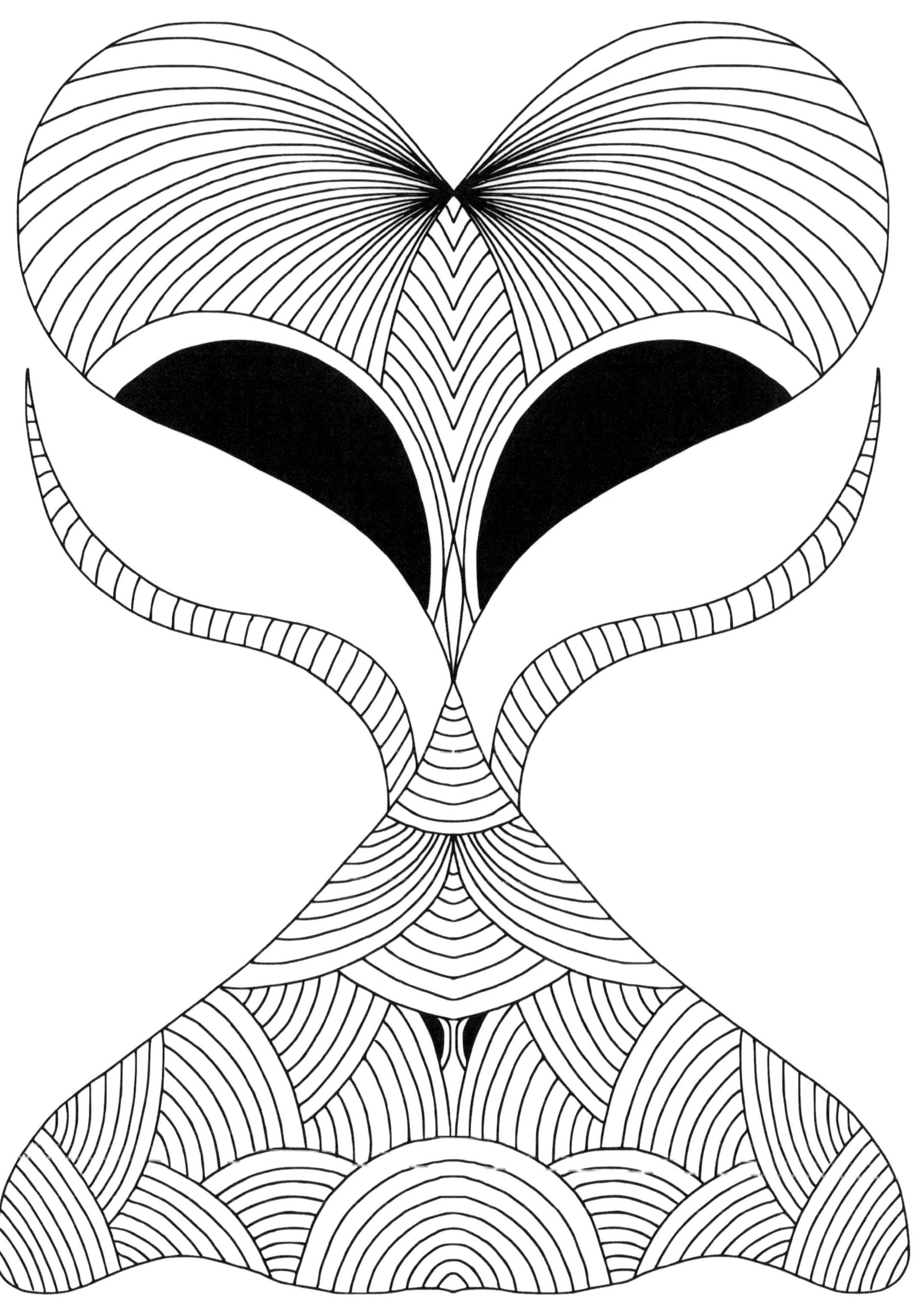

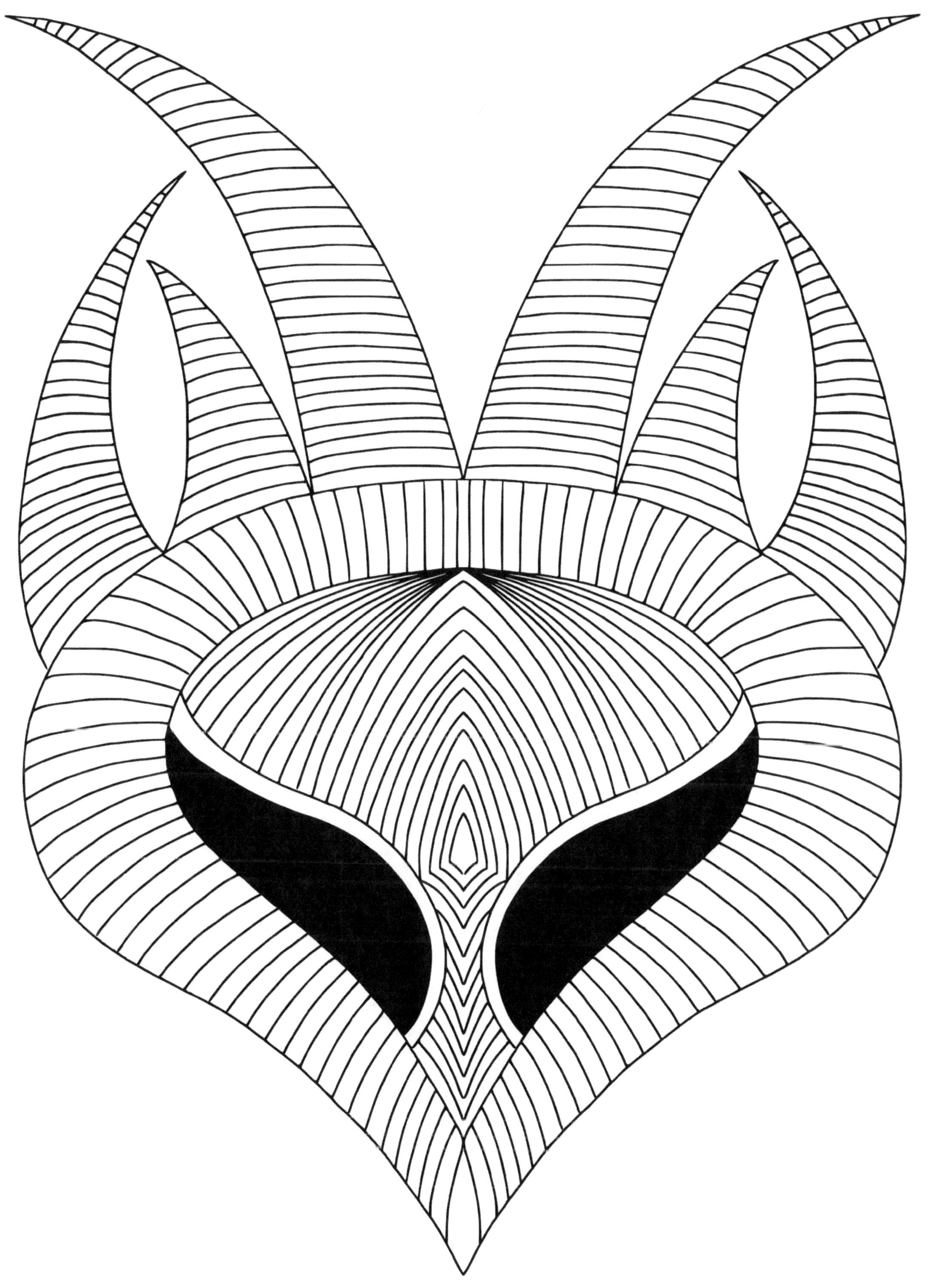

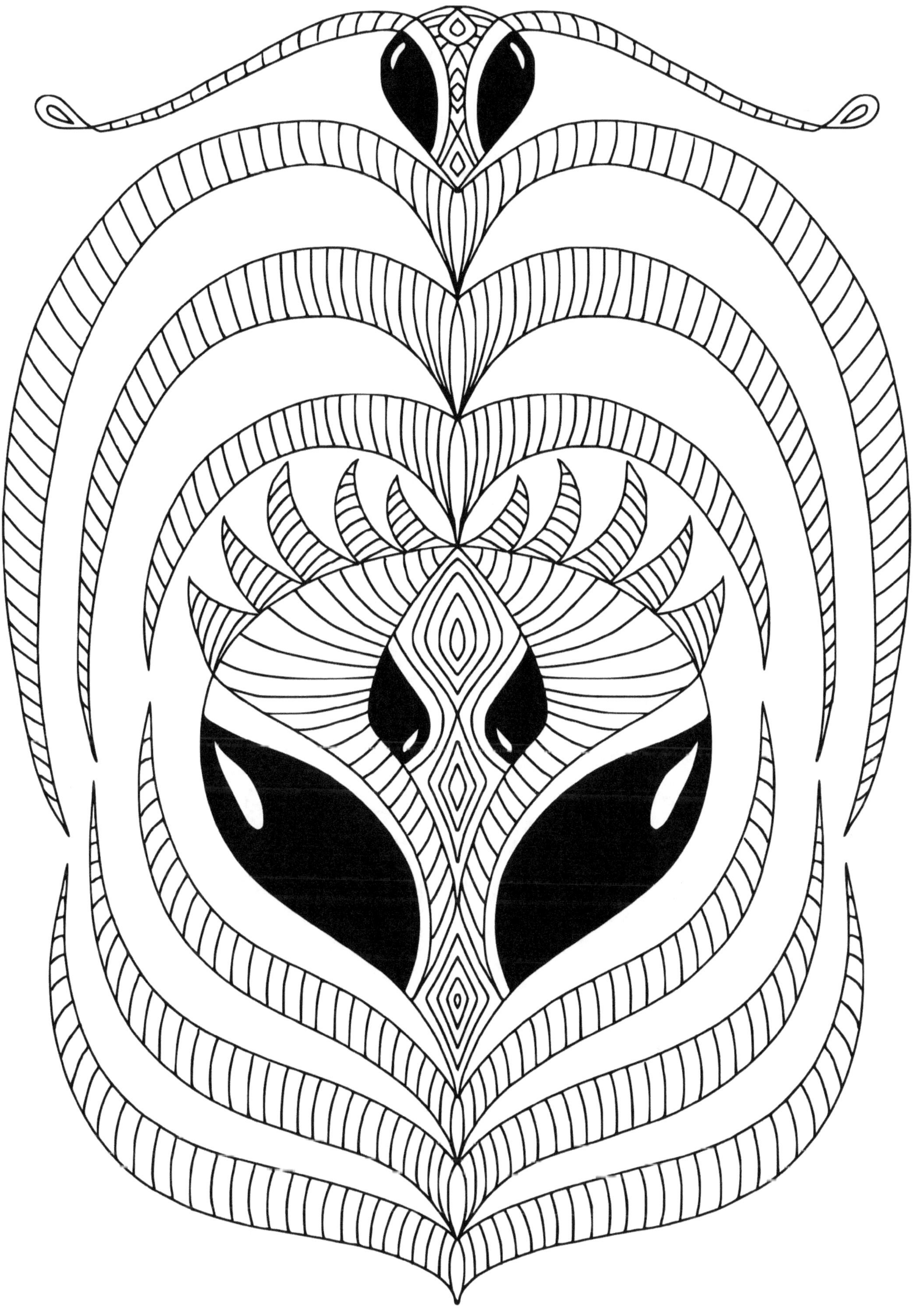

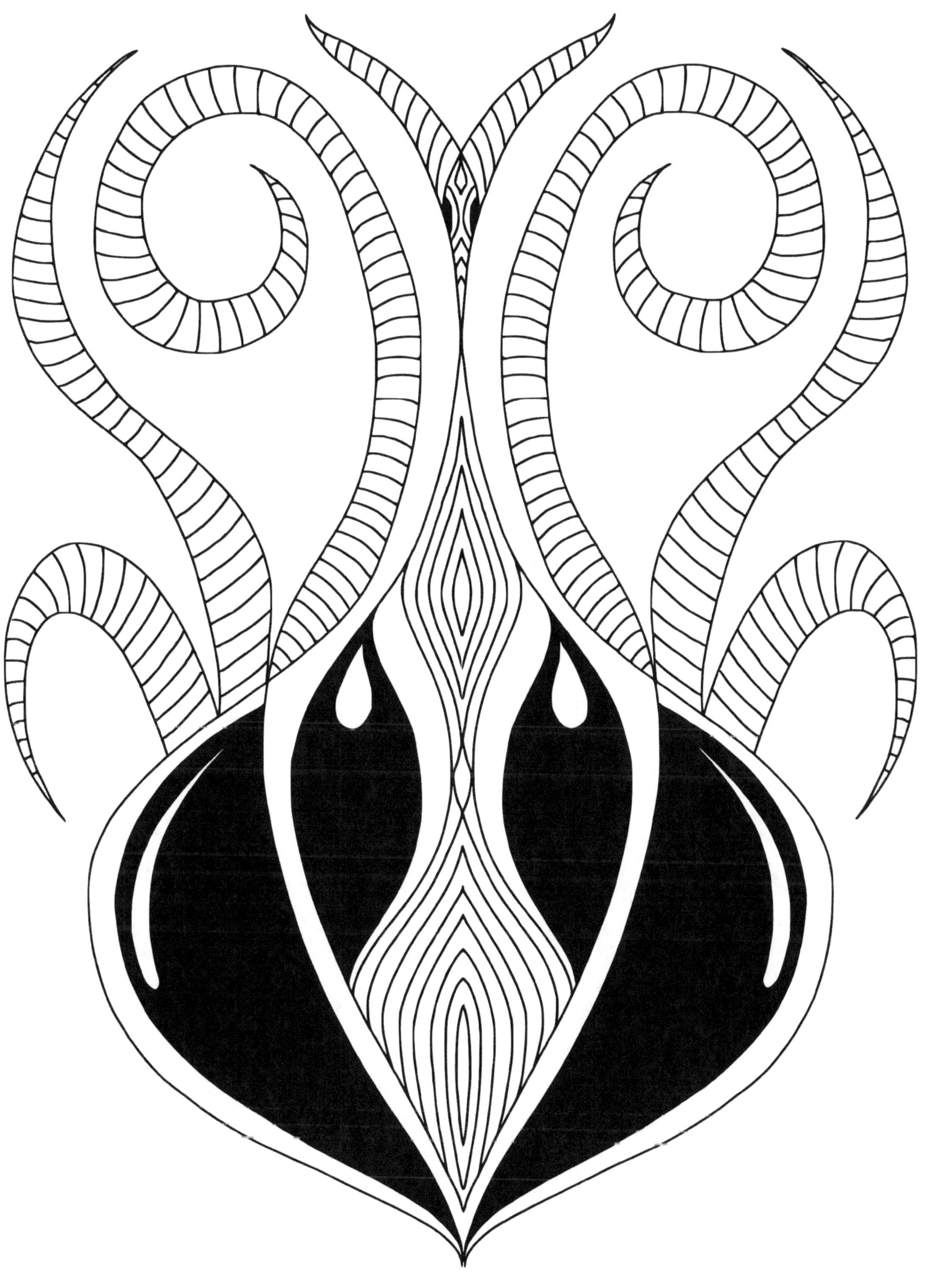

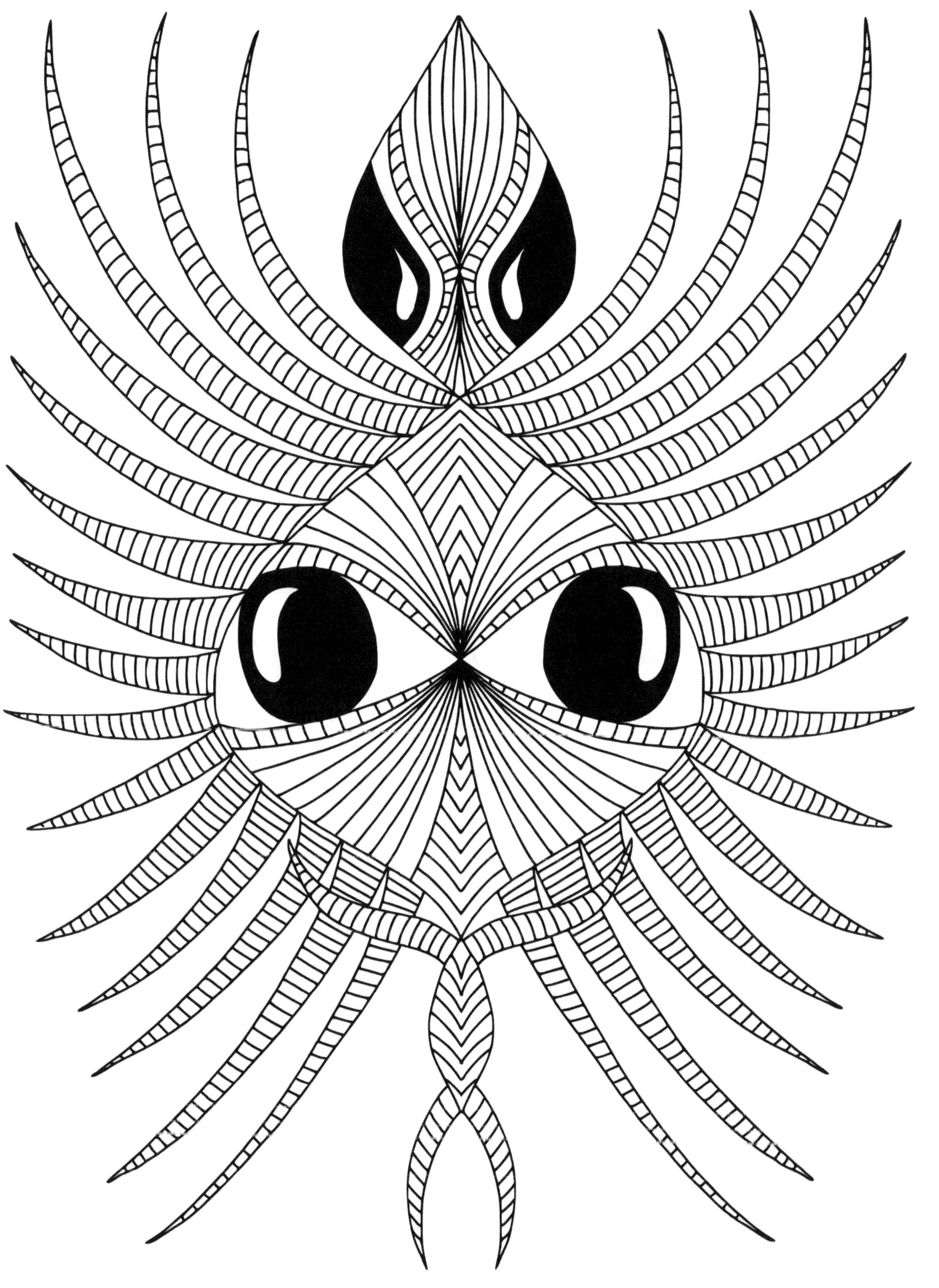

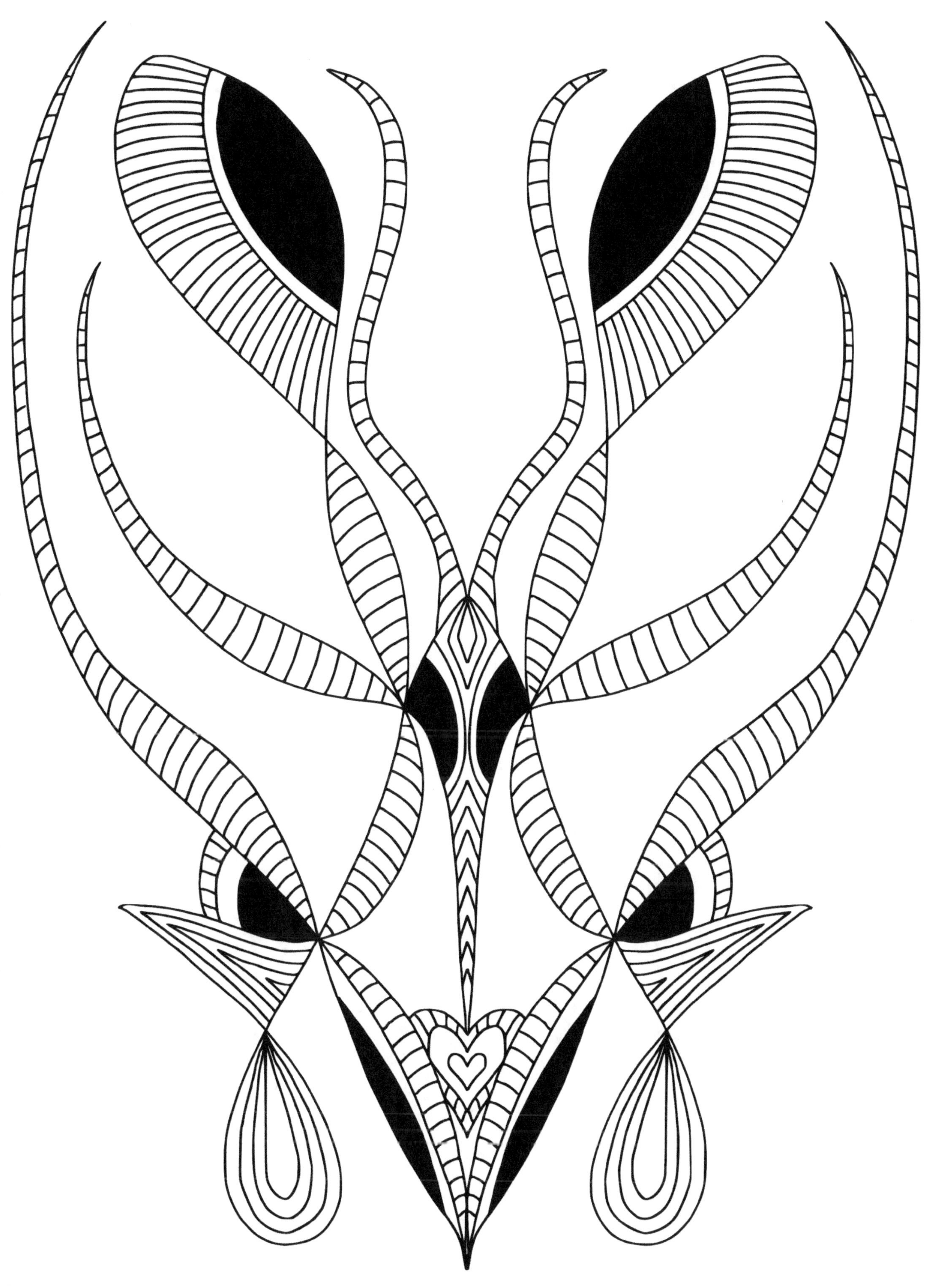

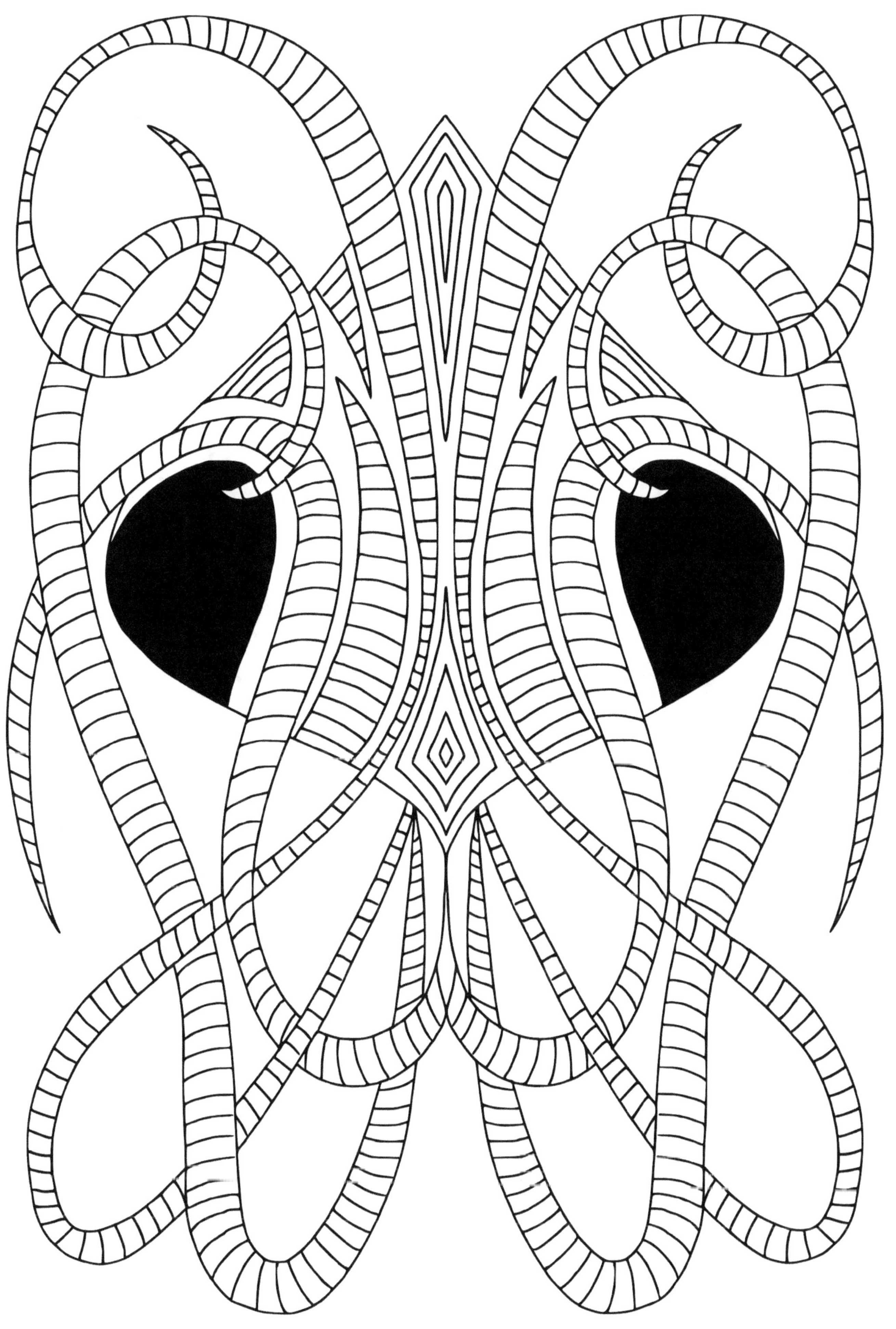

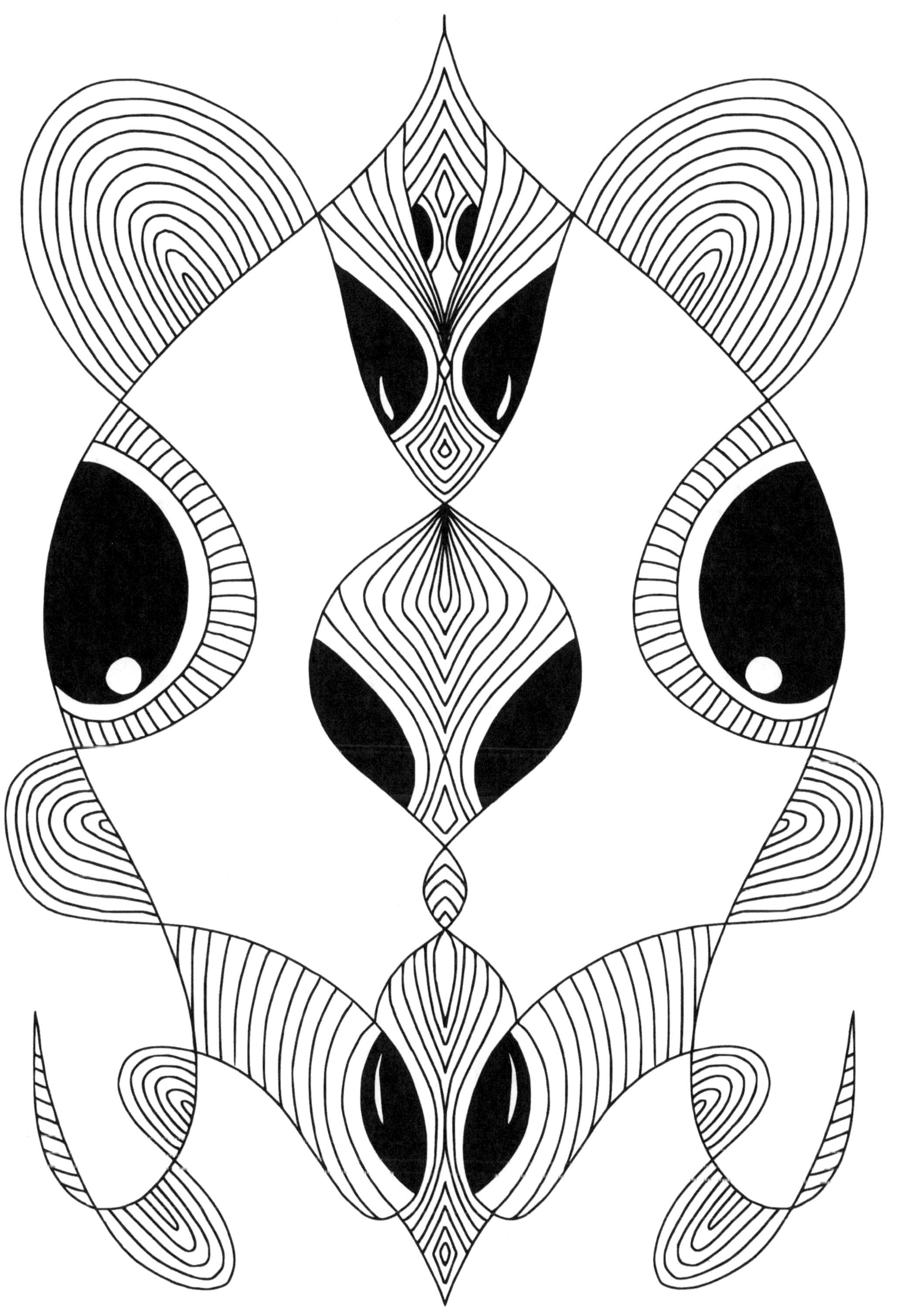

Bonus Upside Down versions......

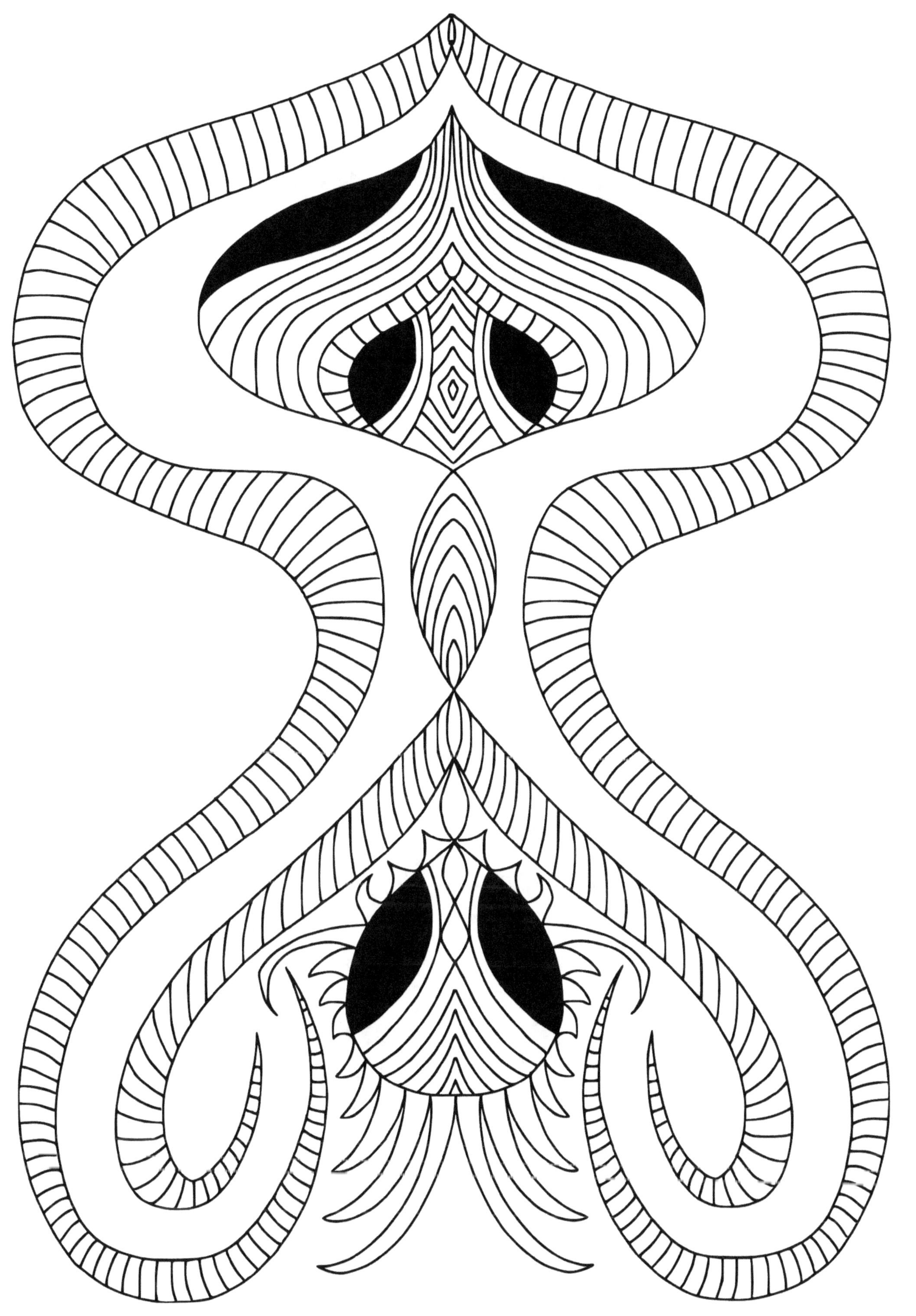

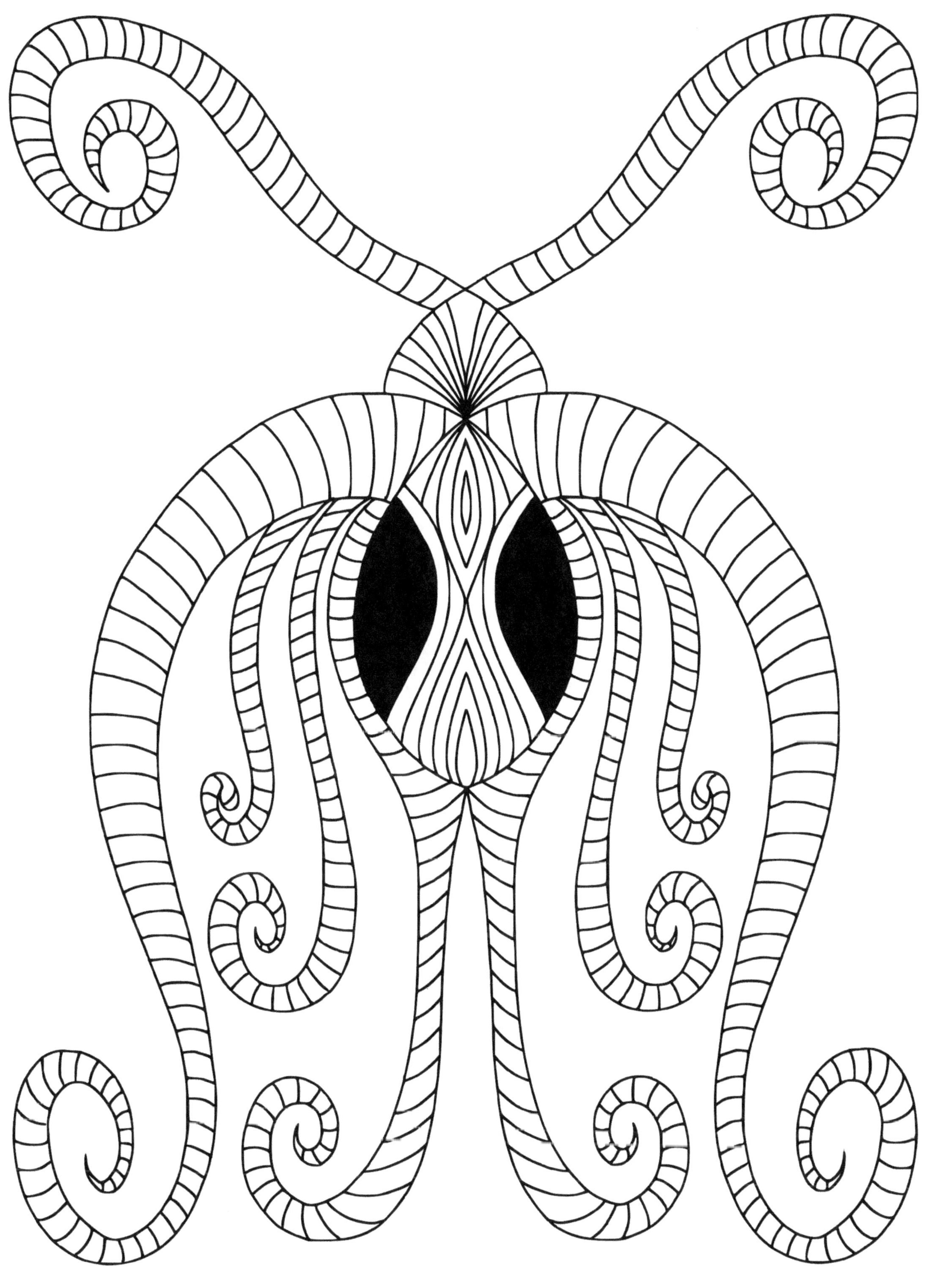

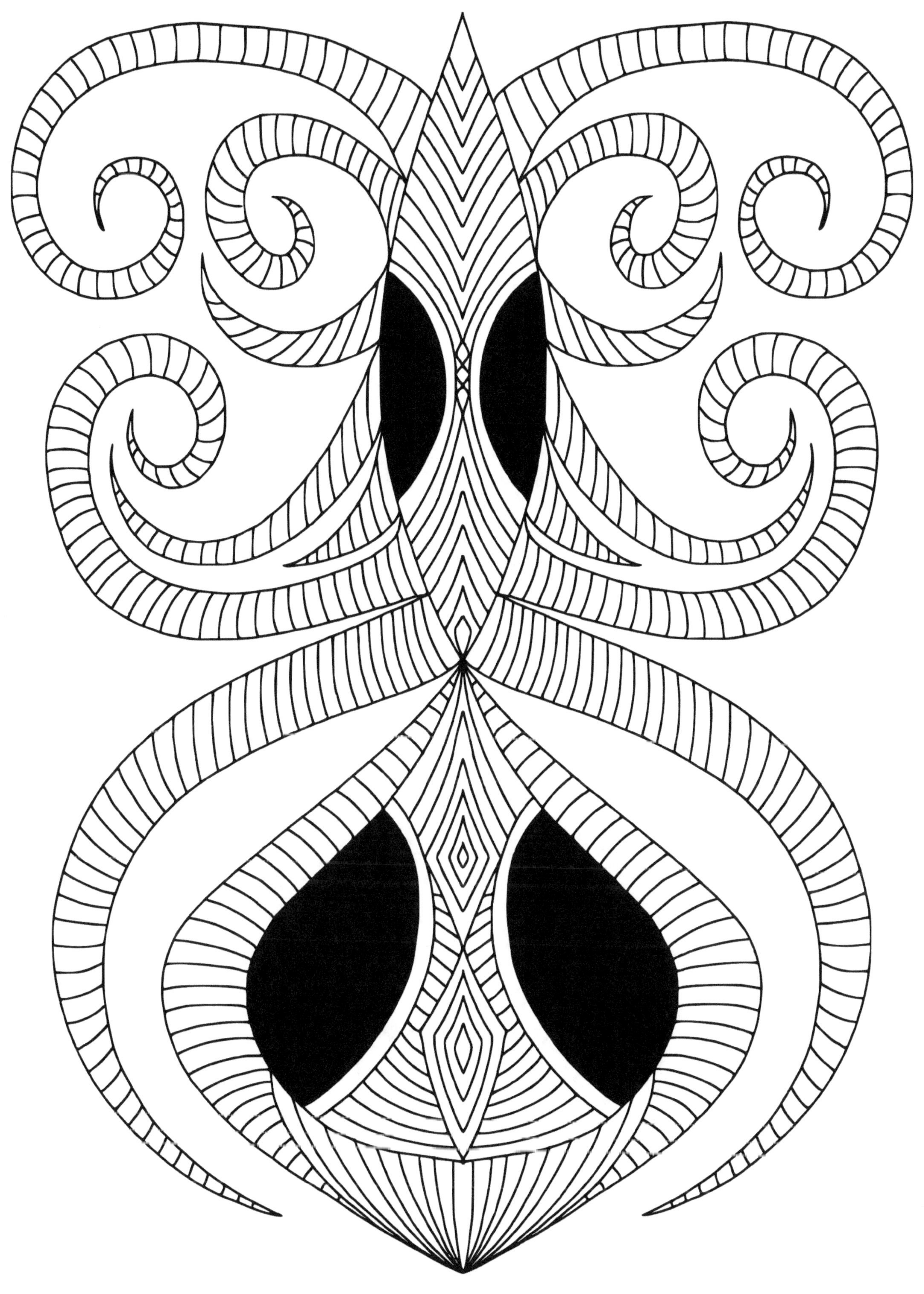

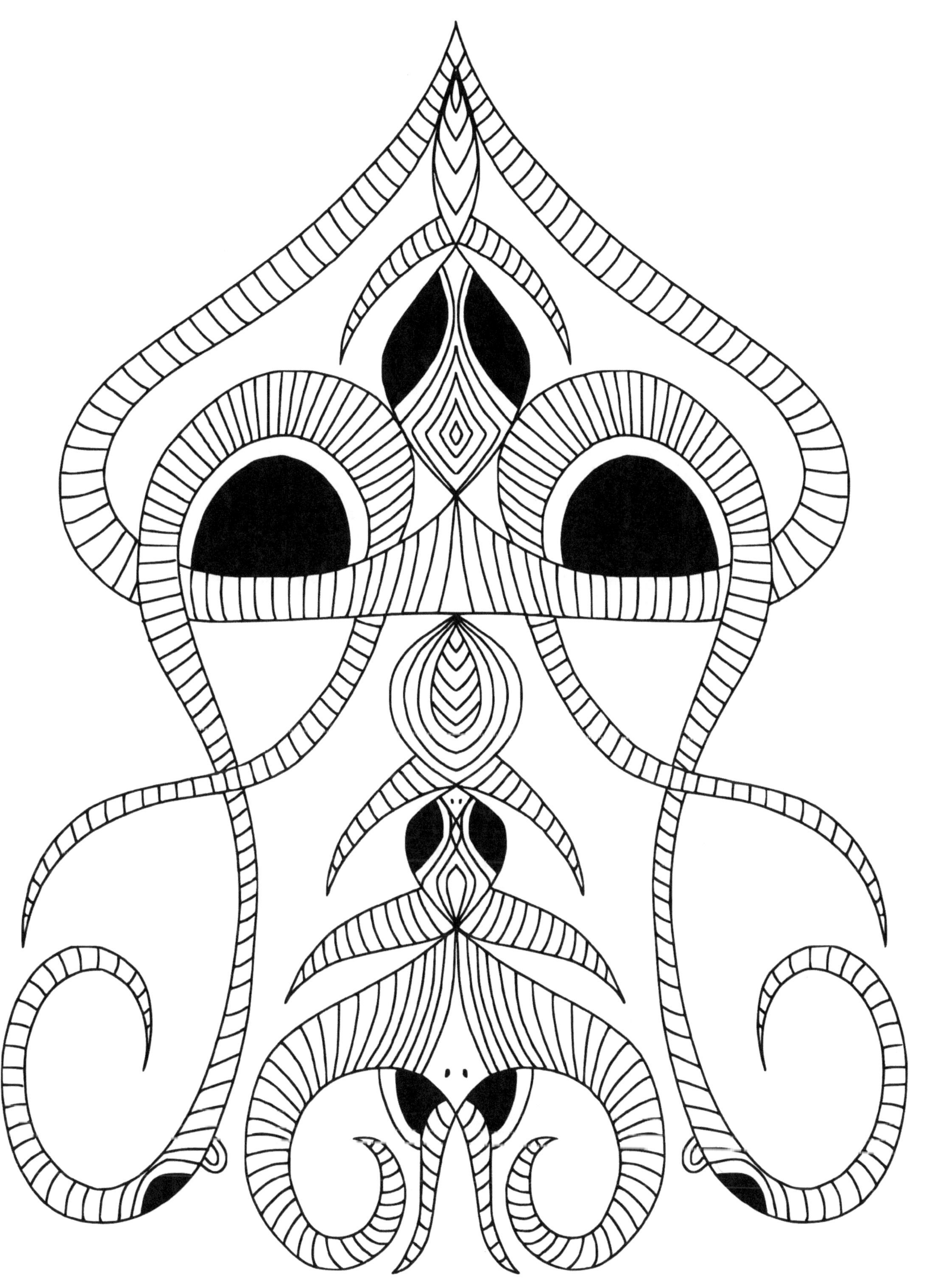

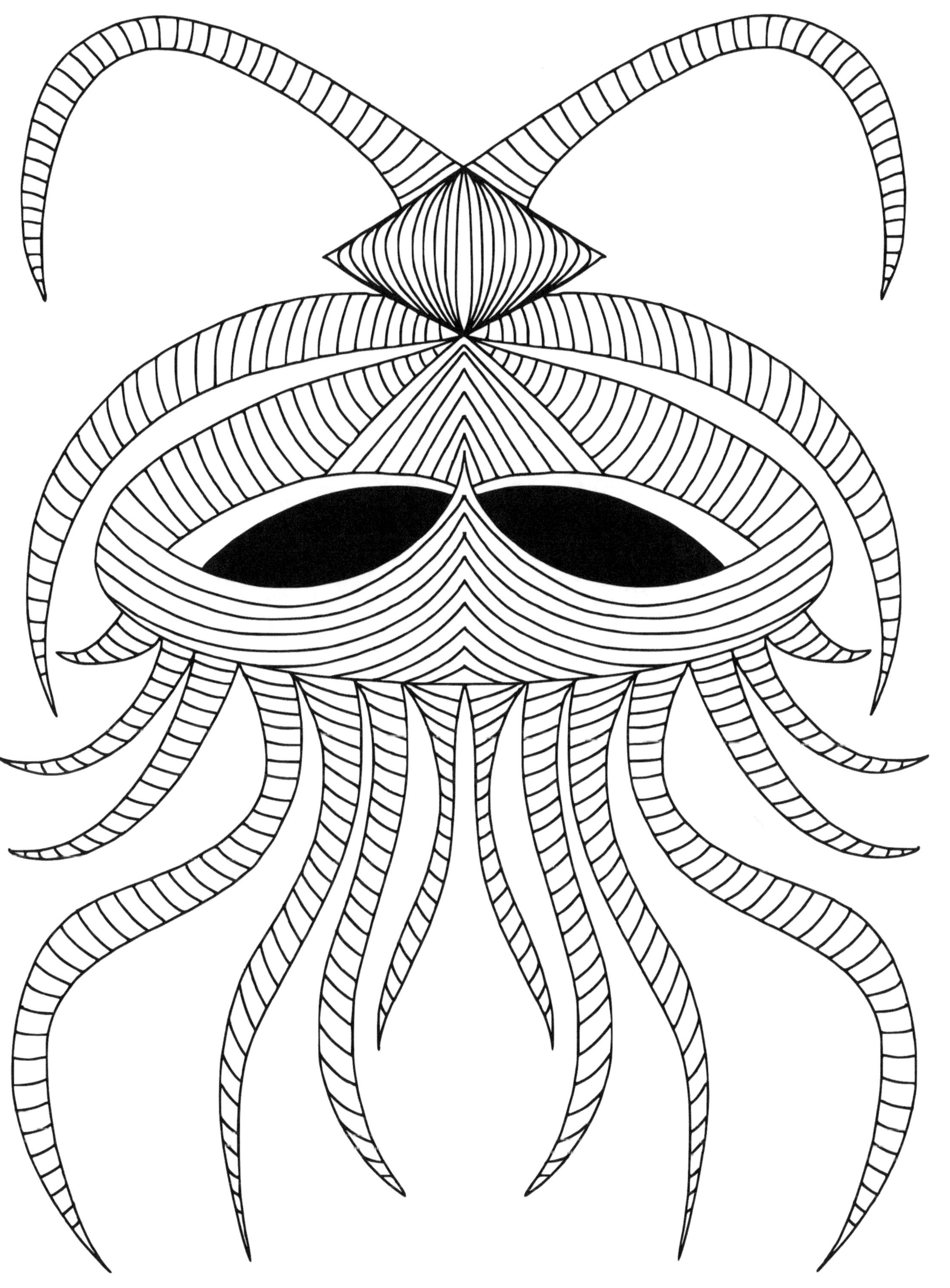

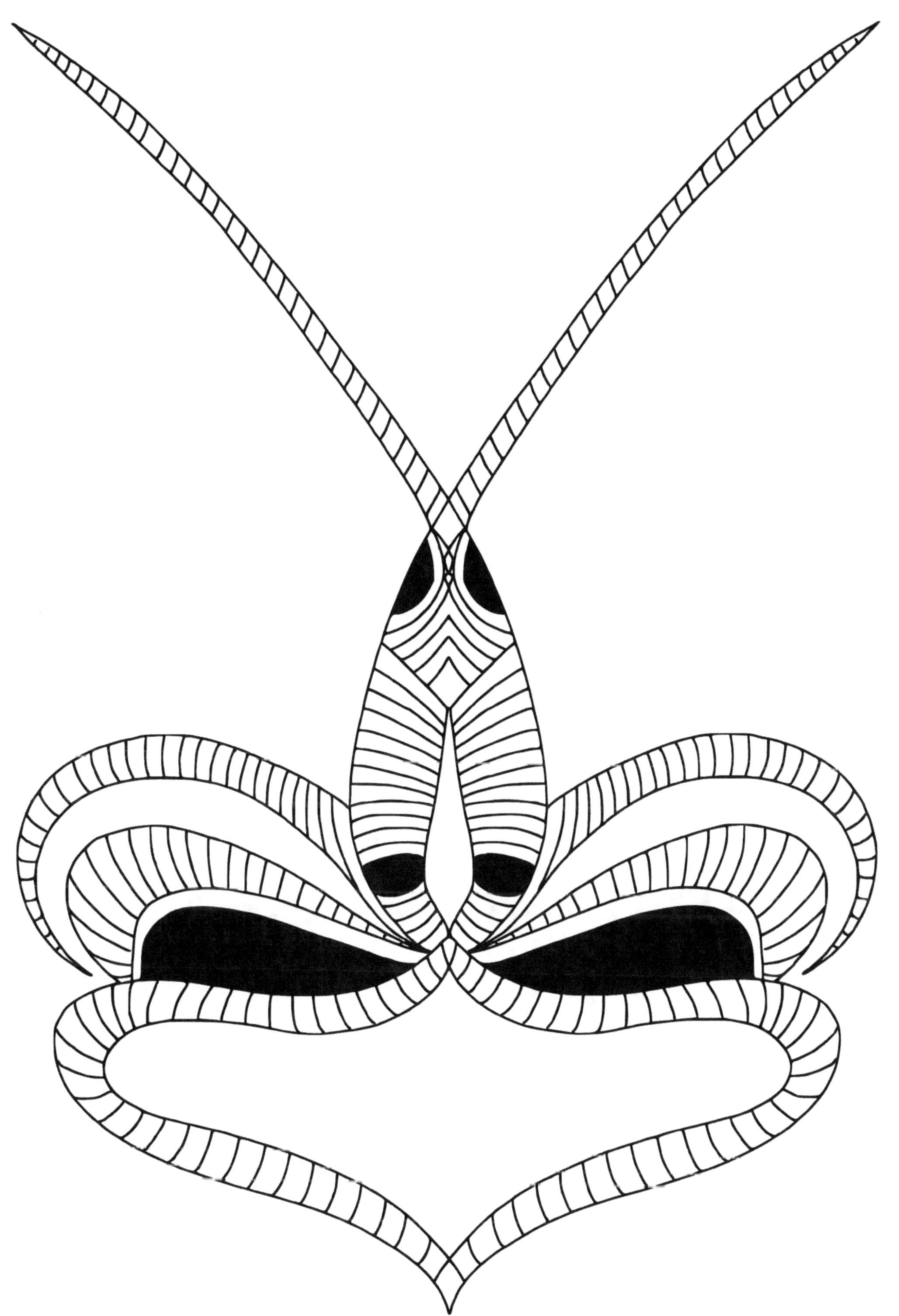

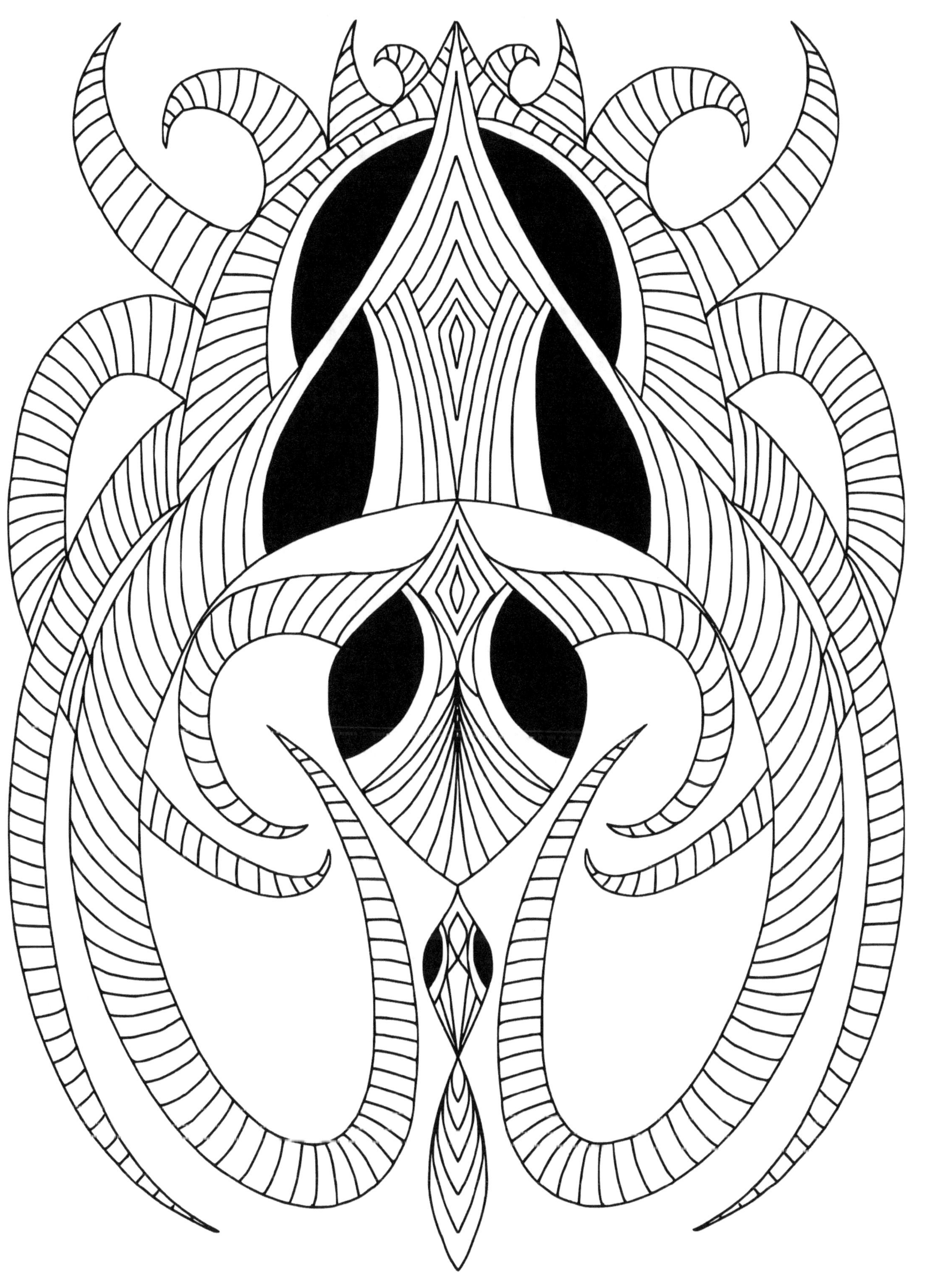

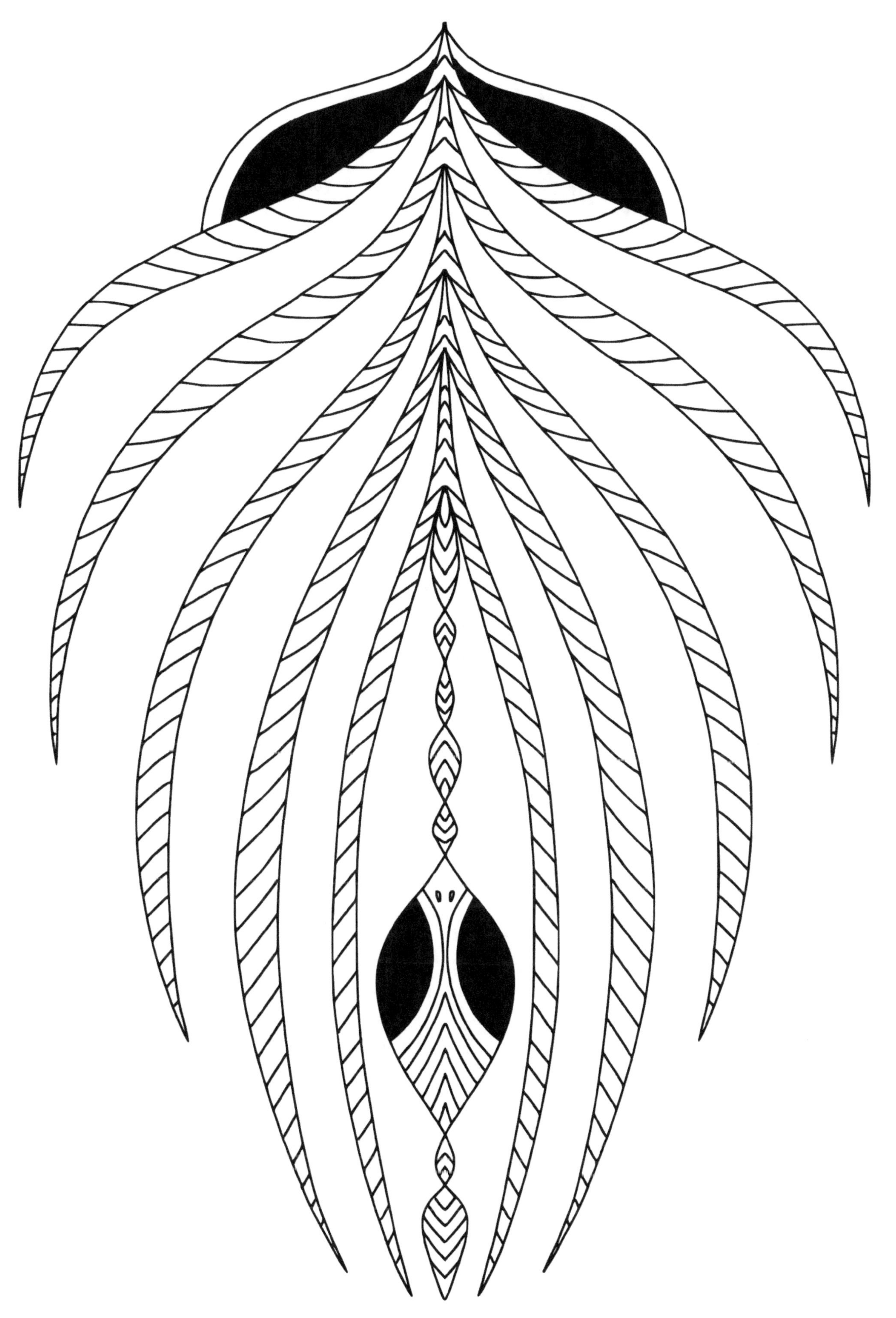

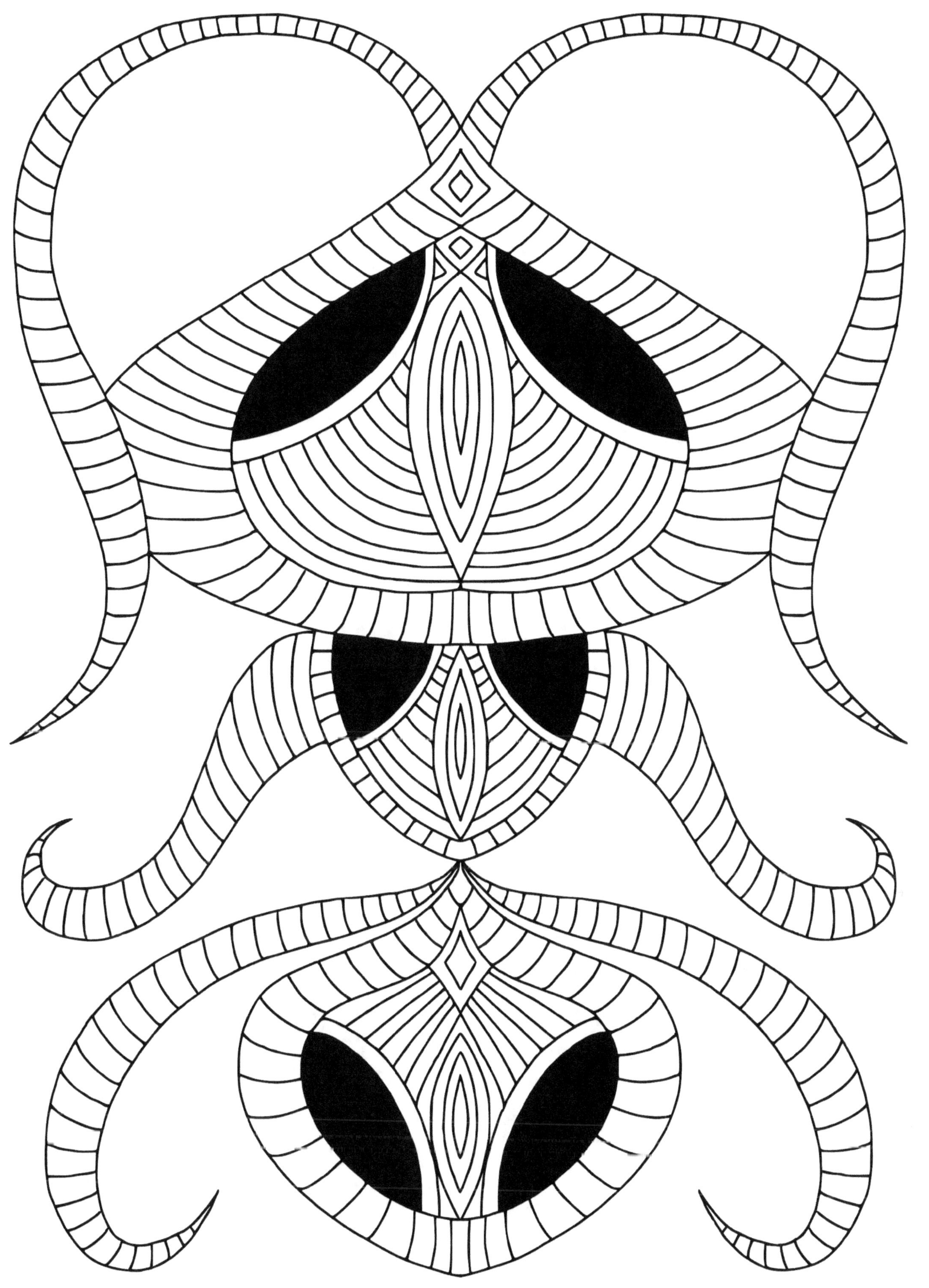

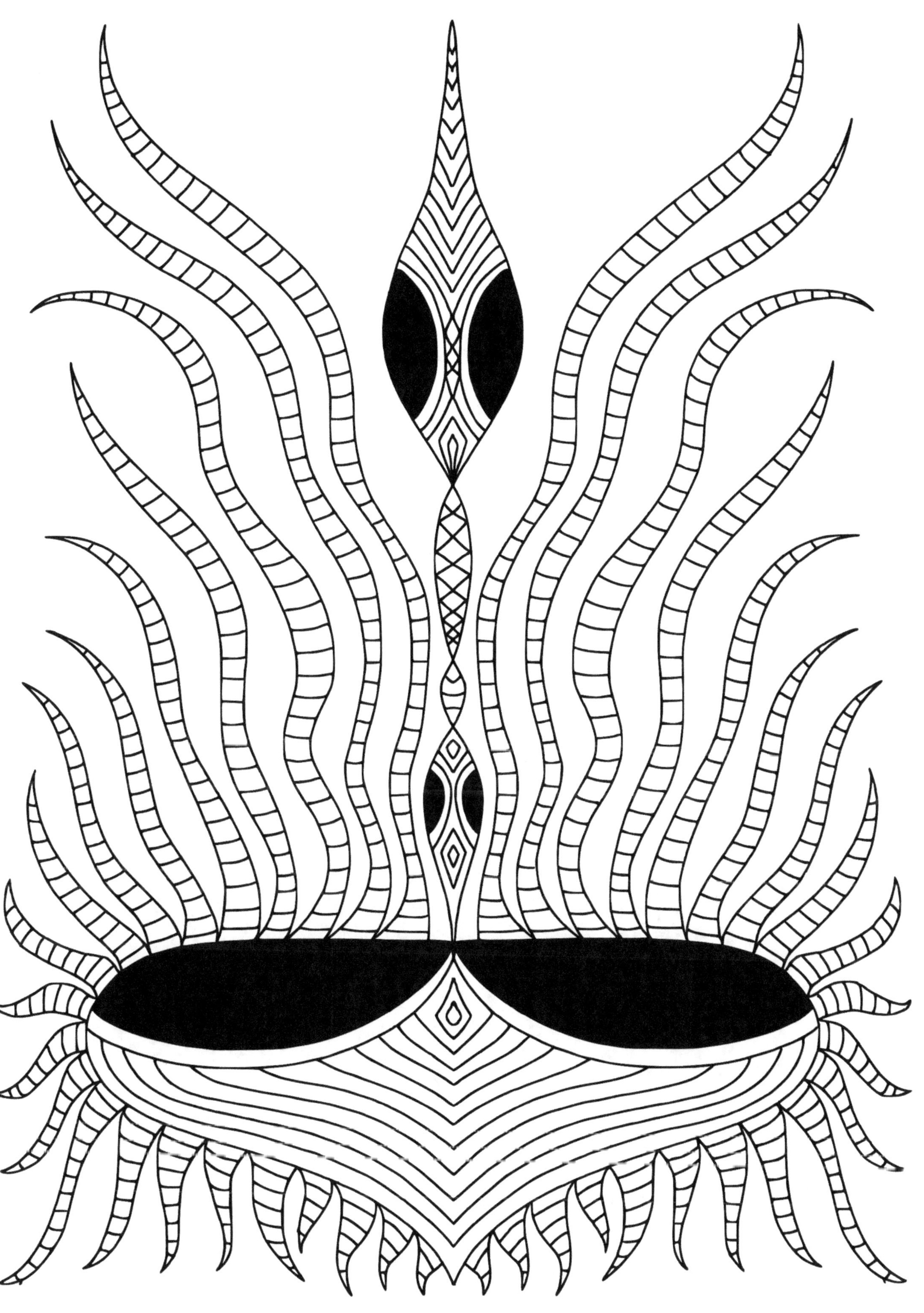

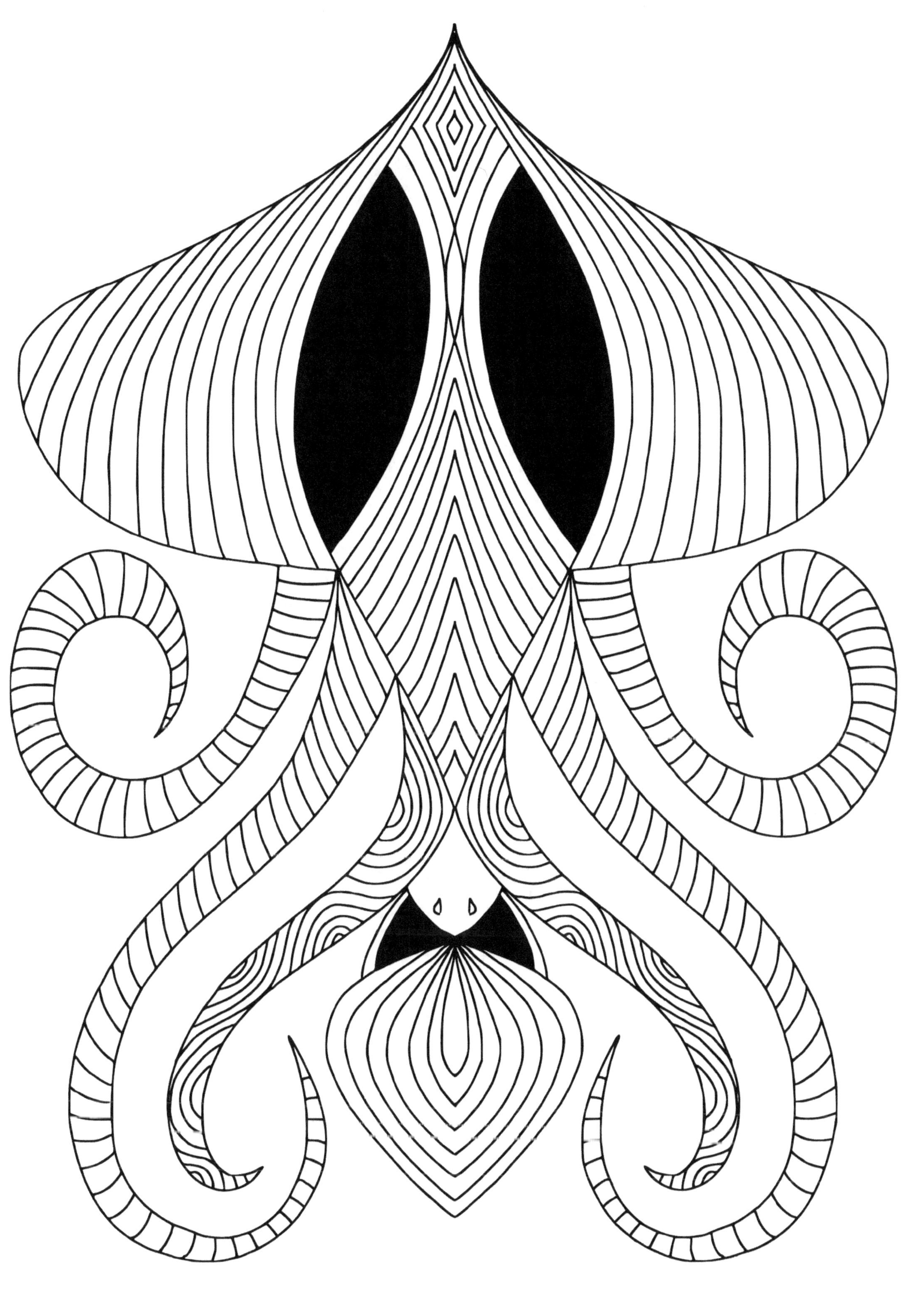

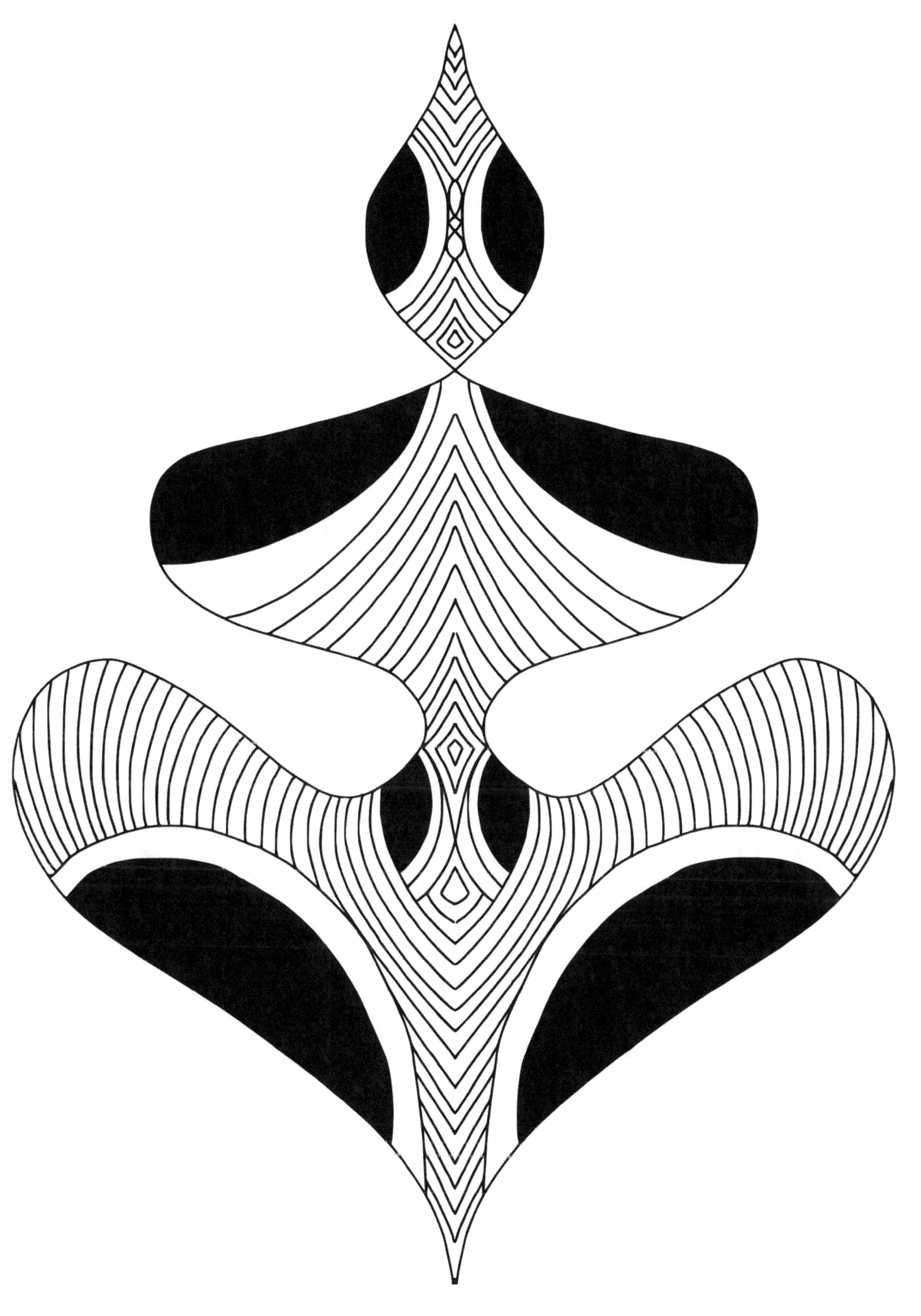

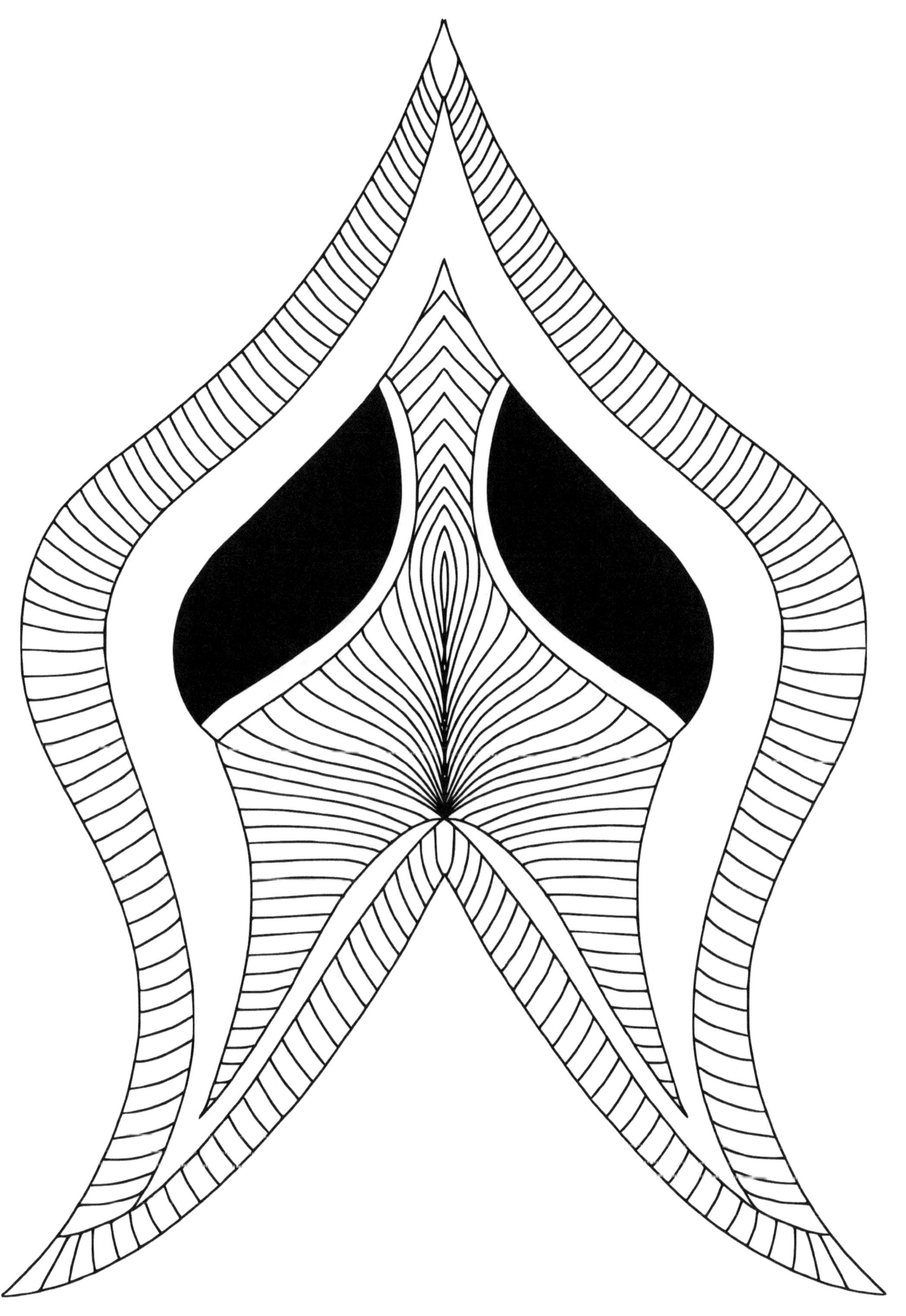

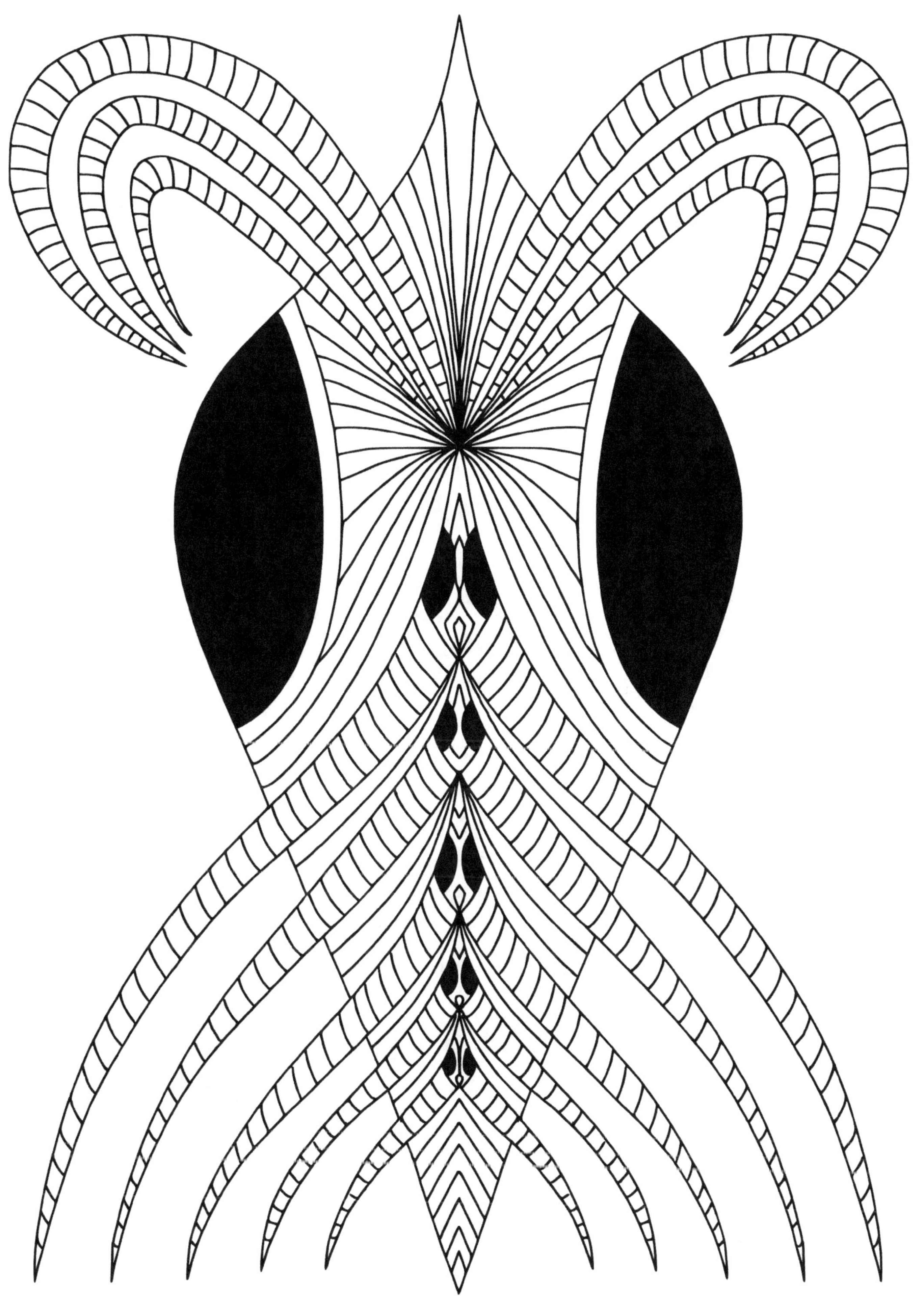

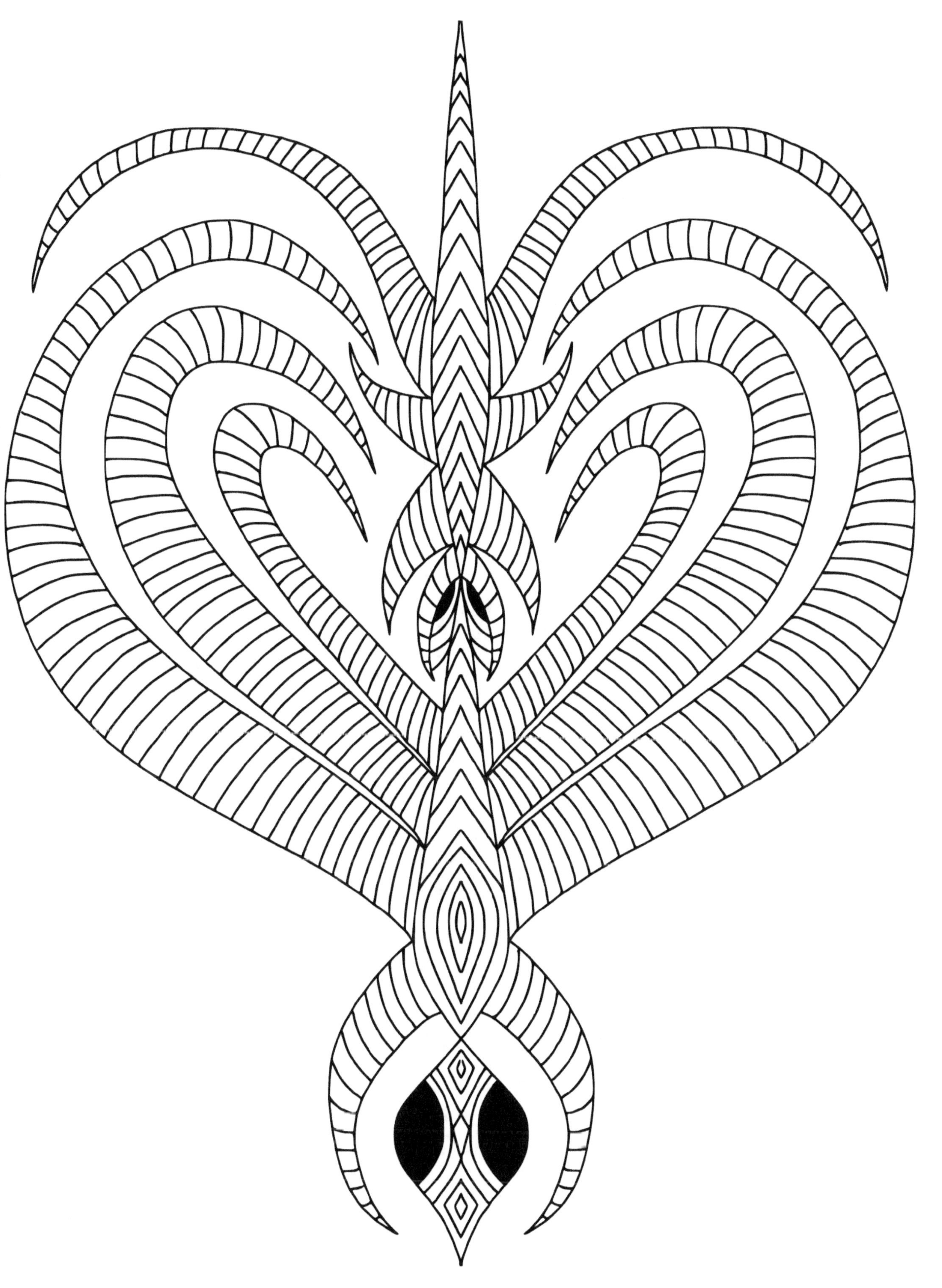

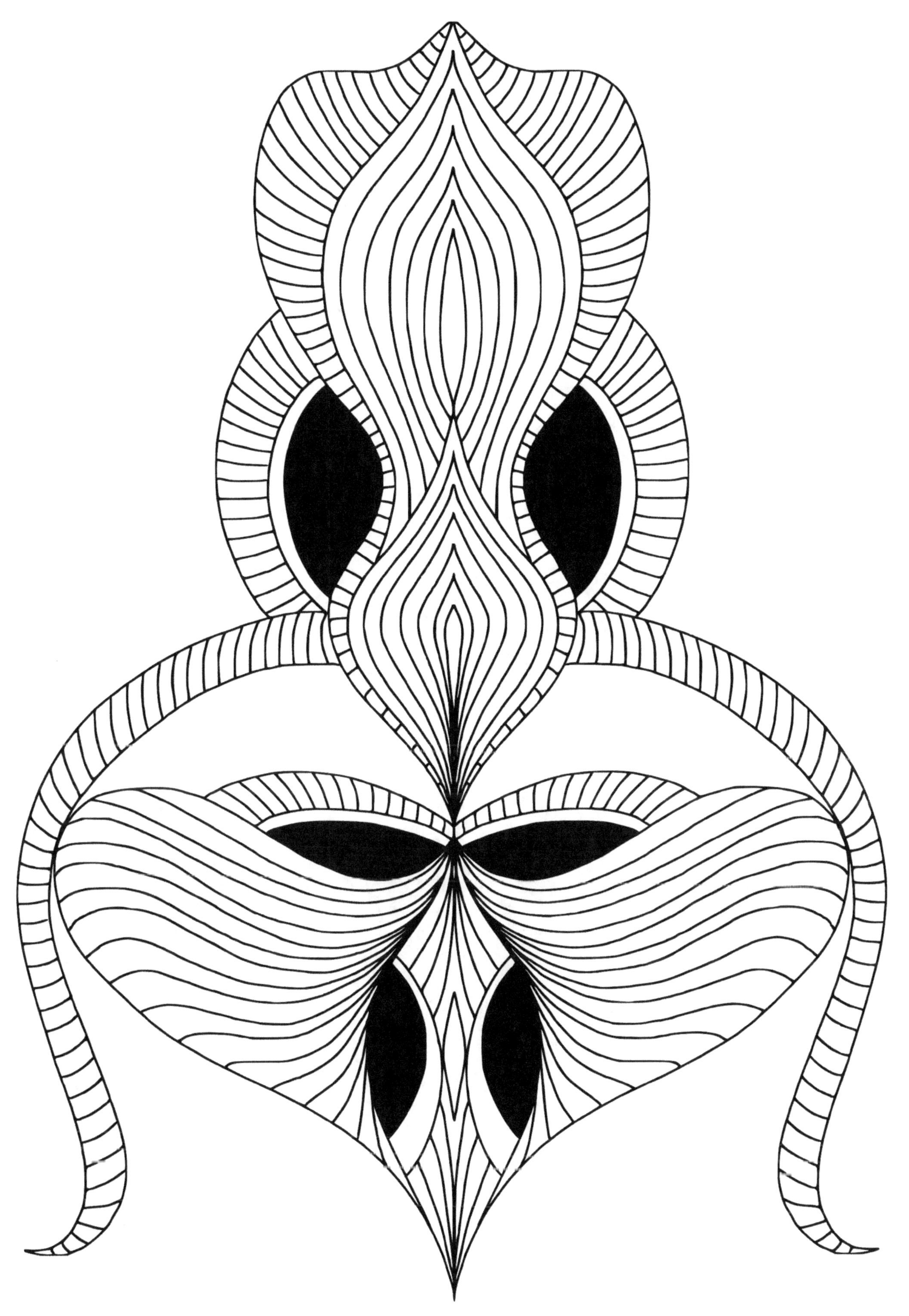

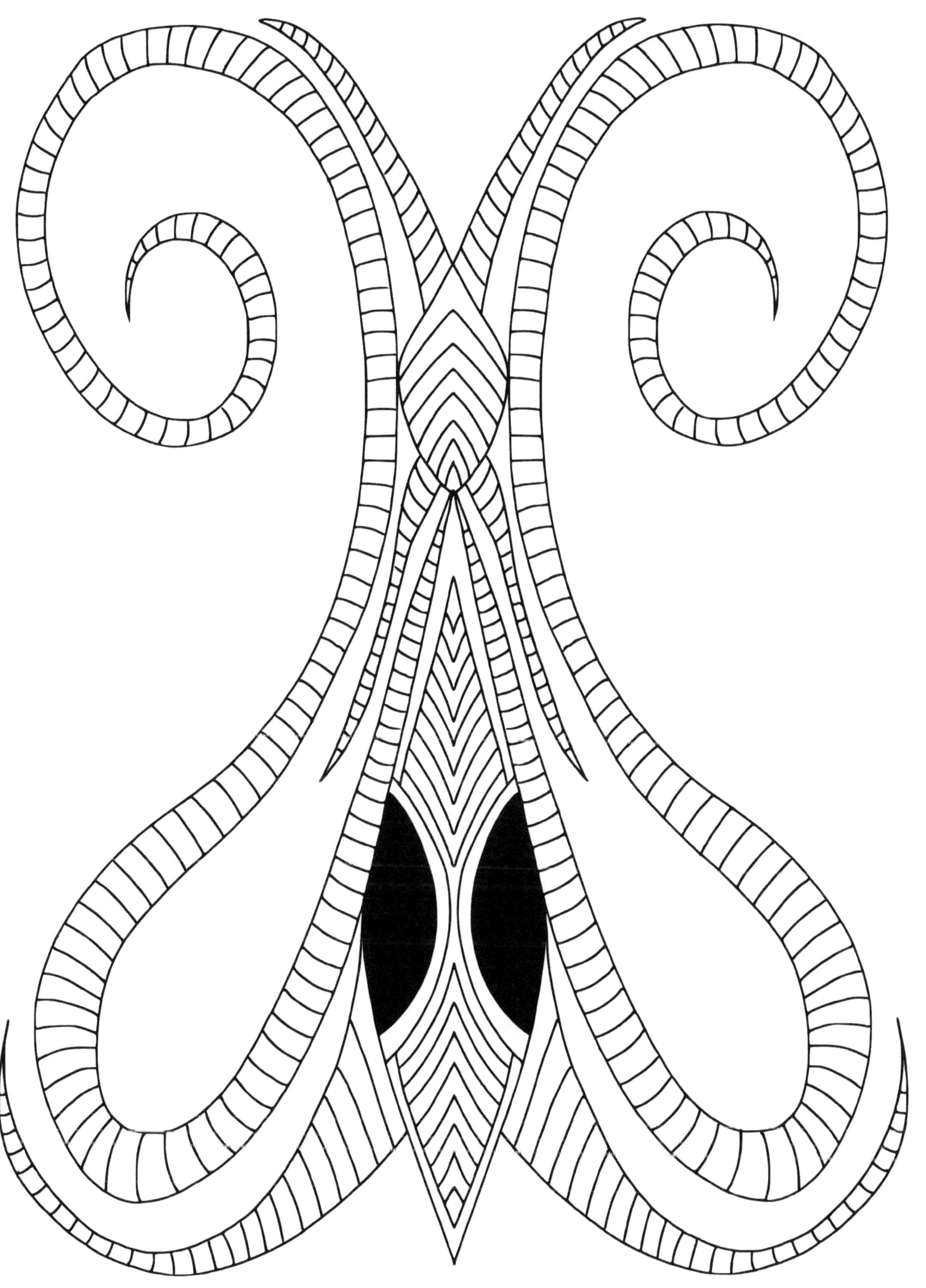

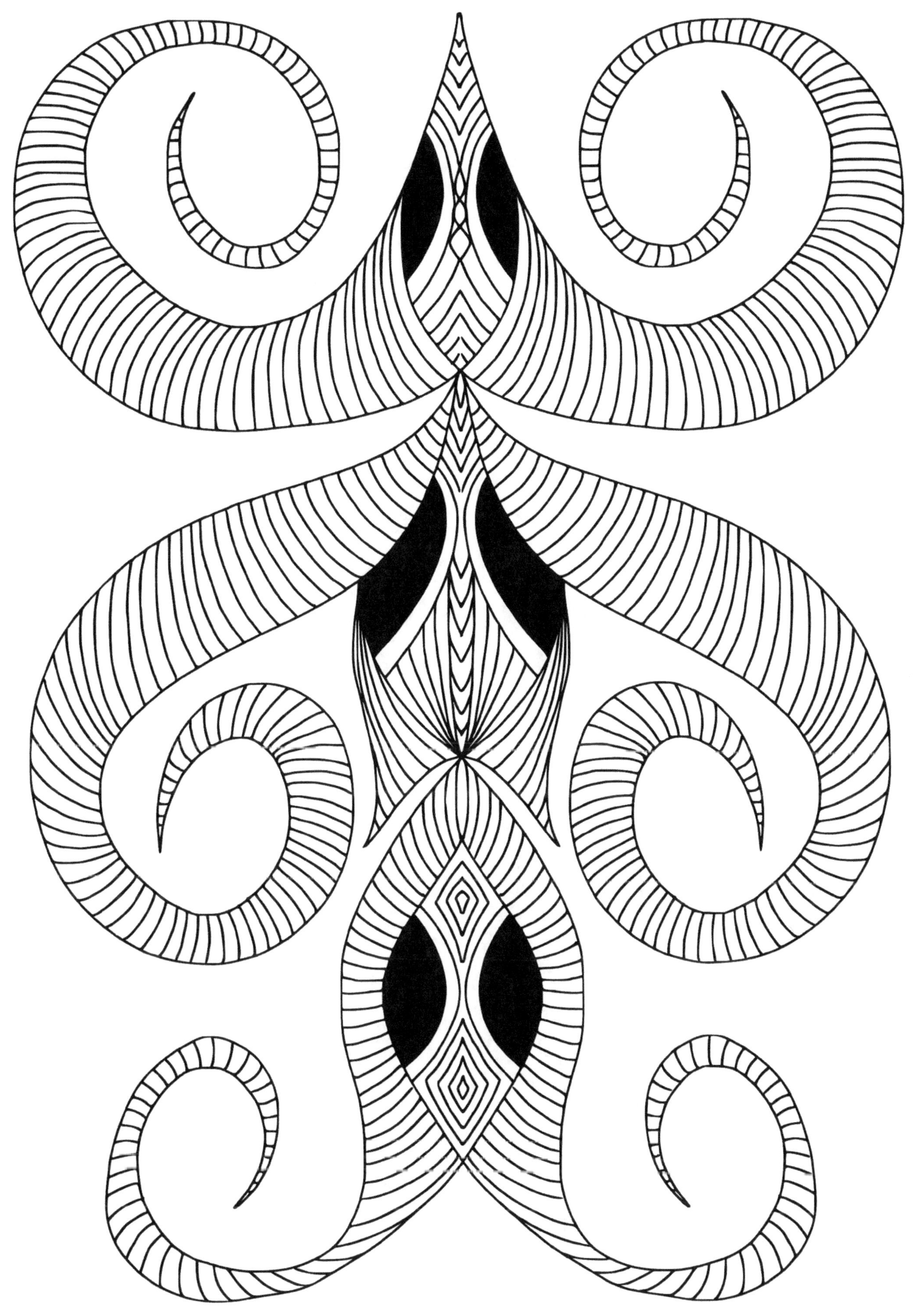

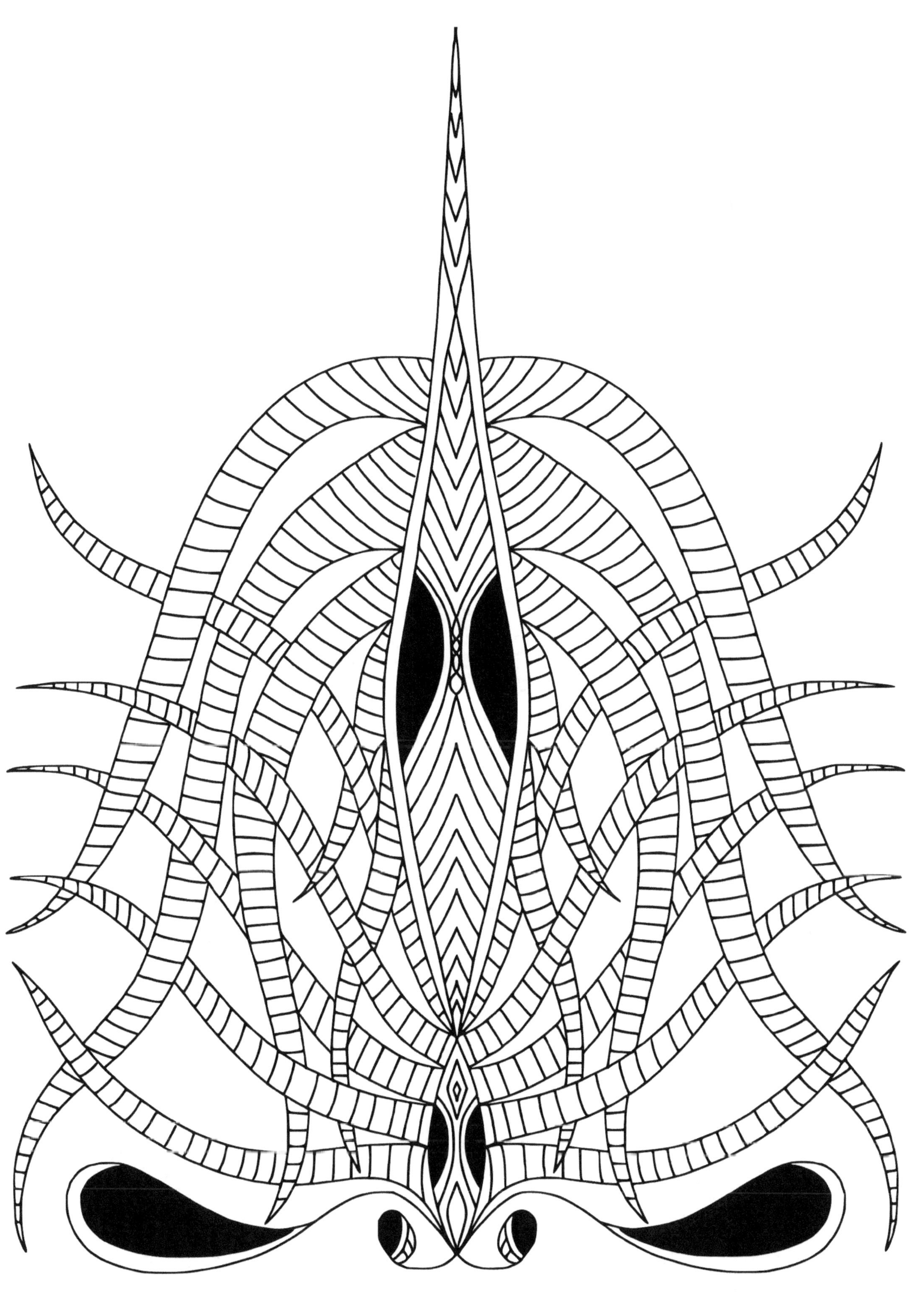

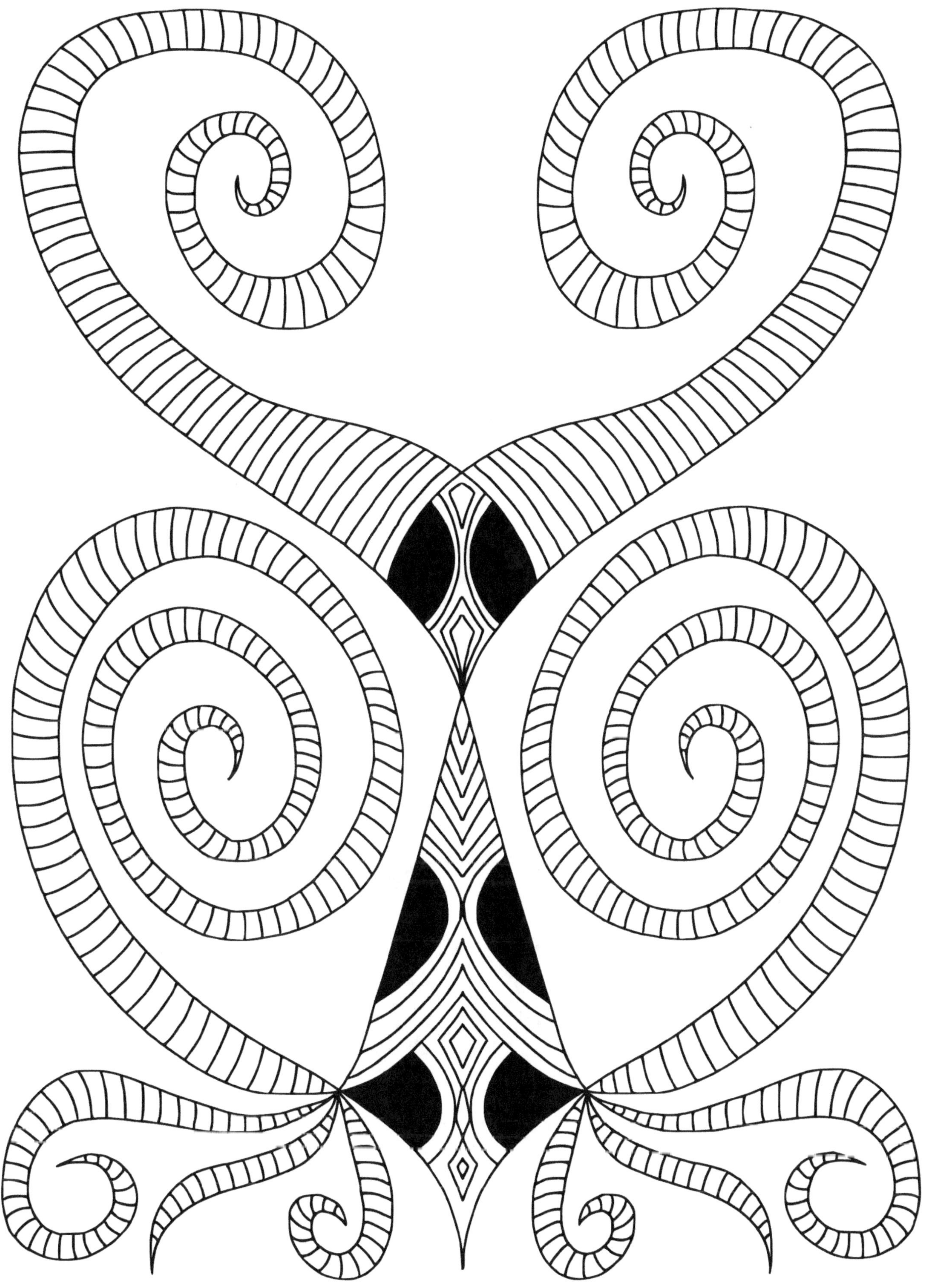

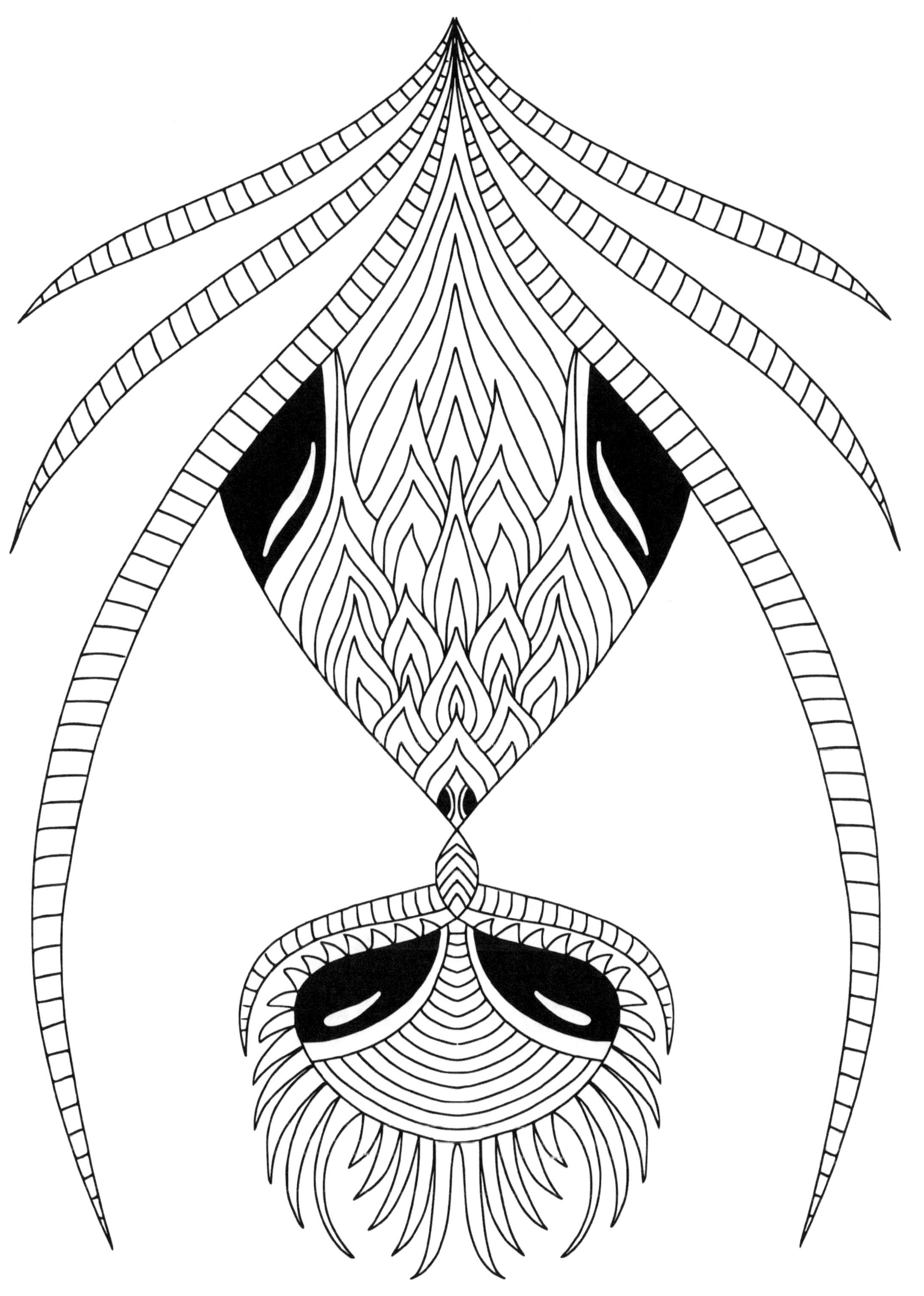

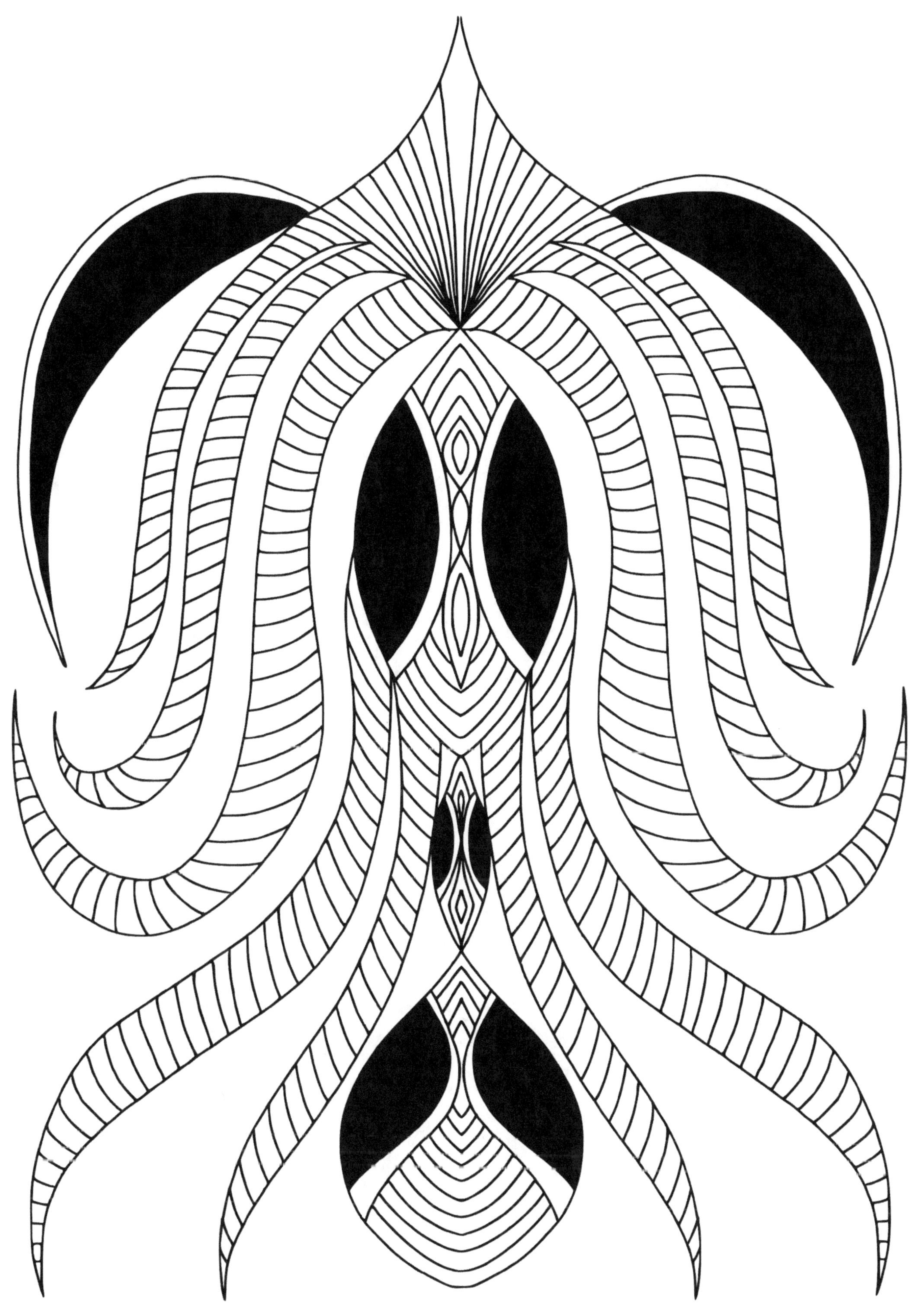

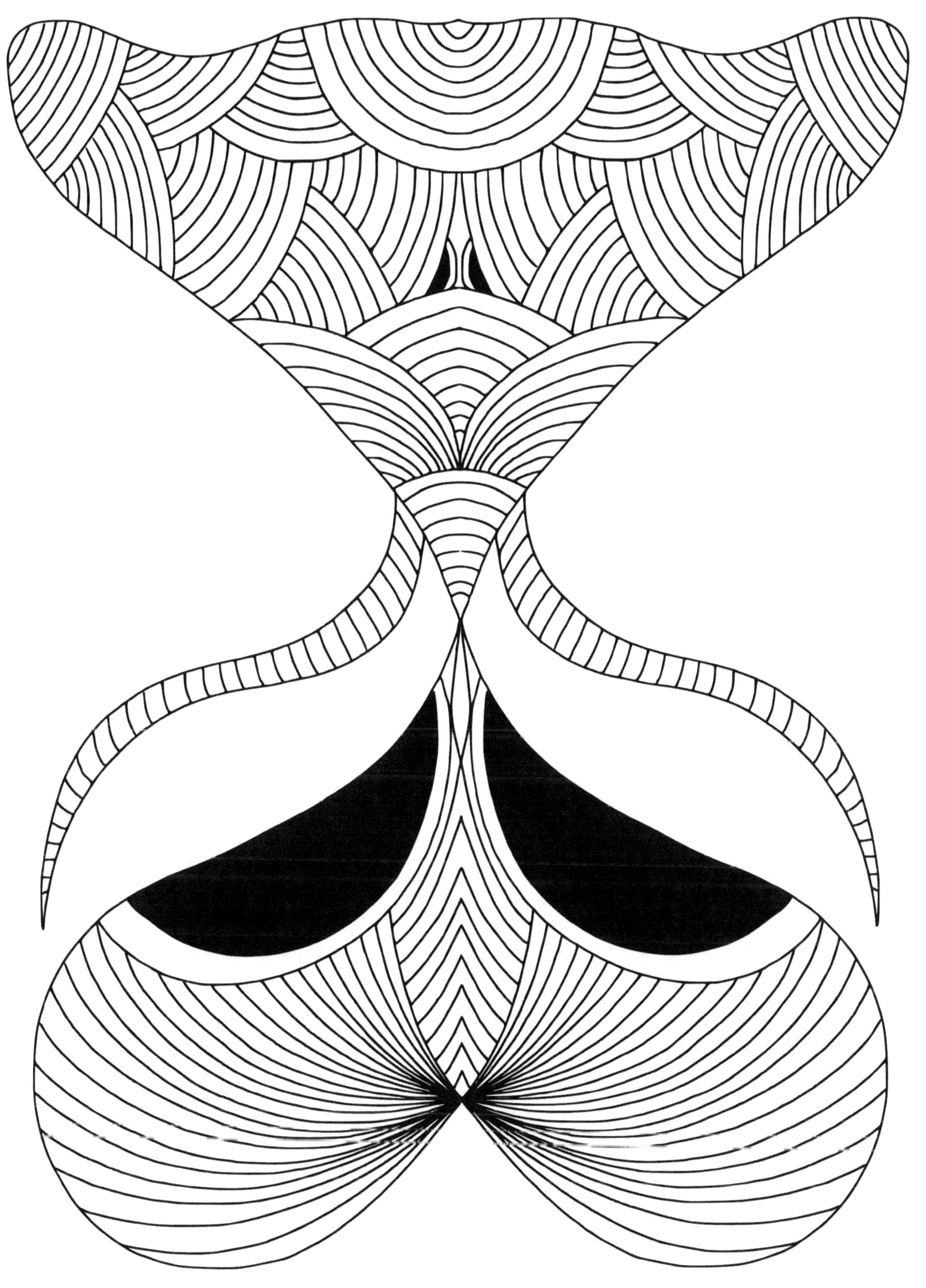

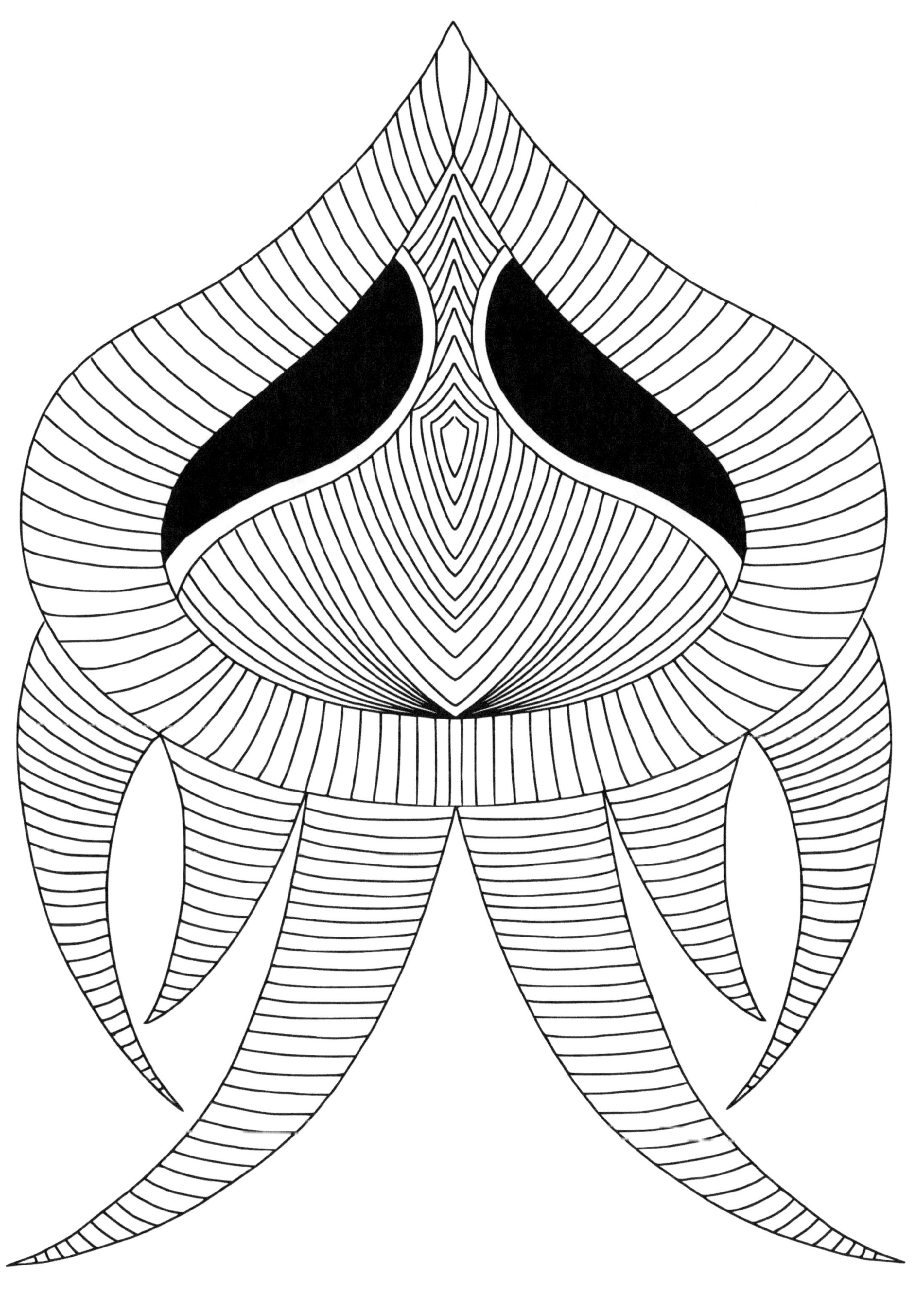

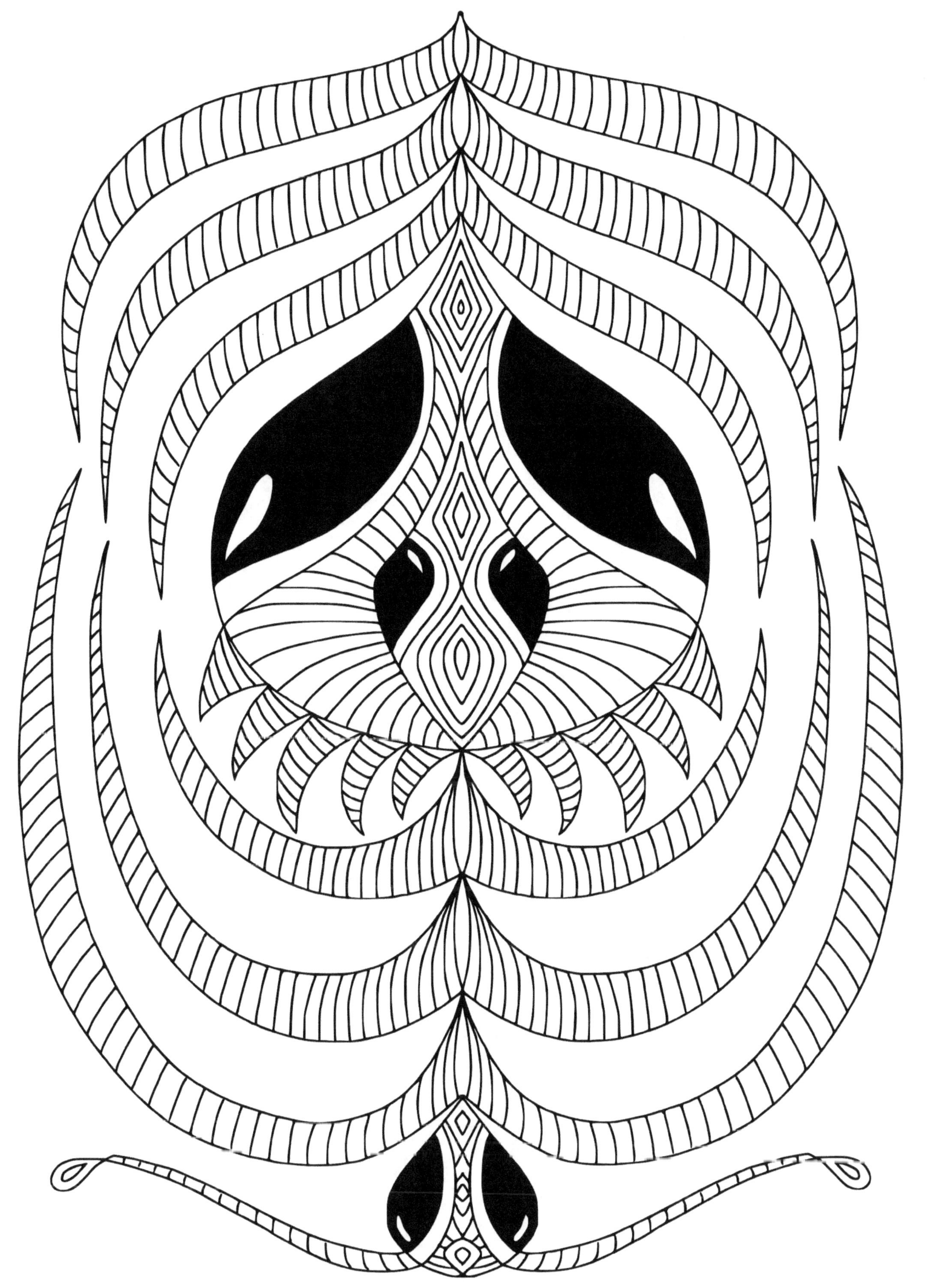

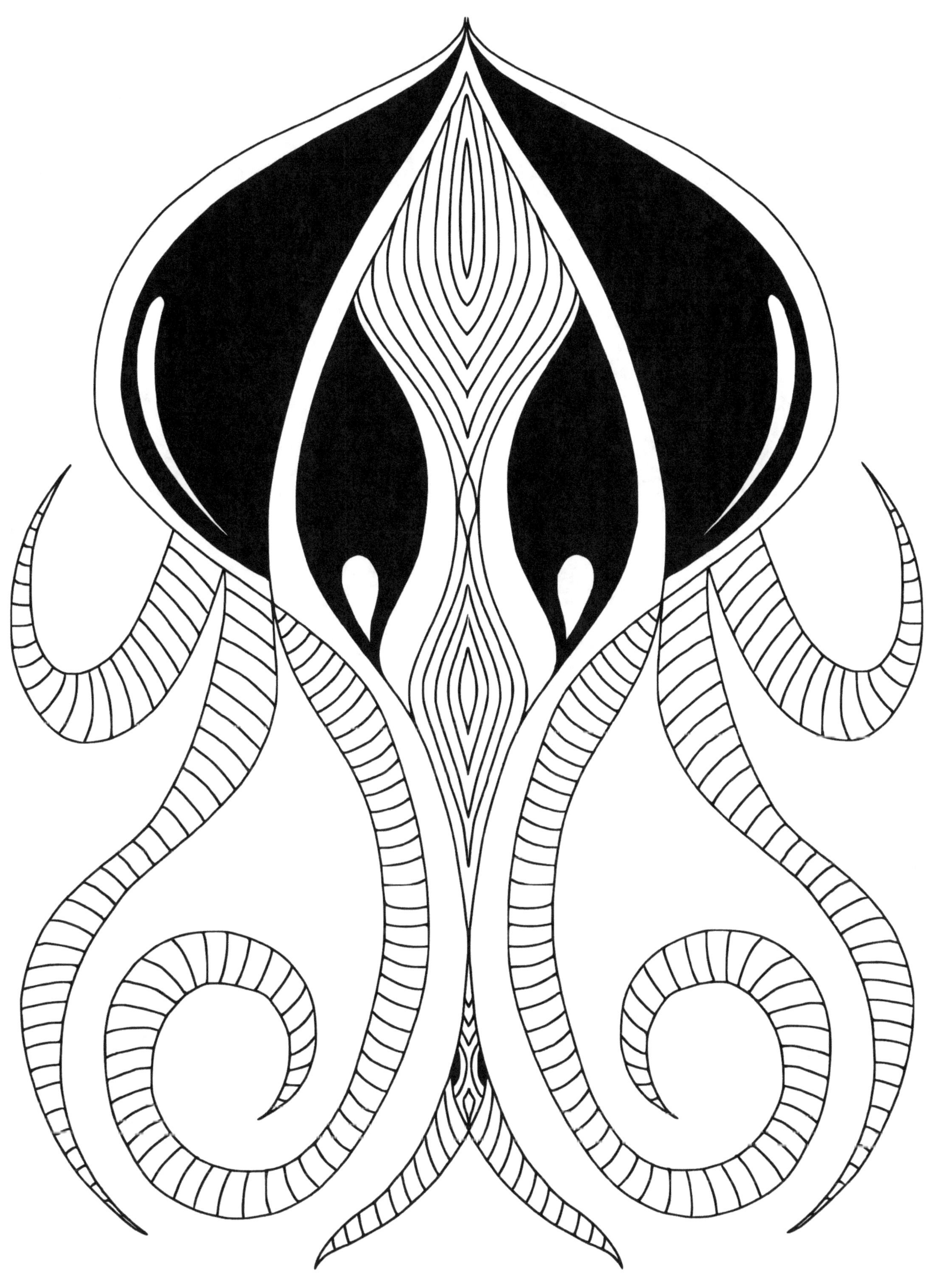

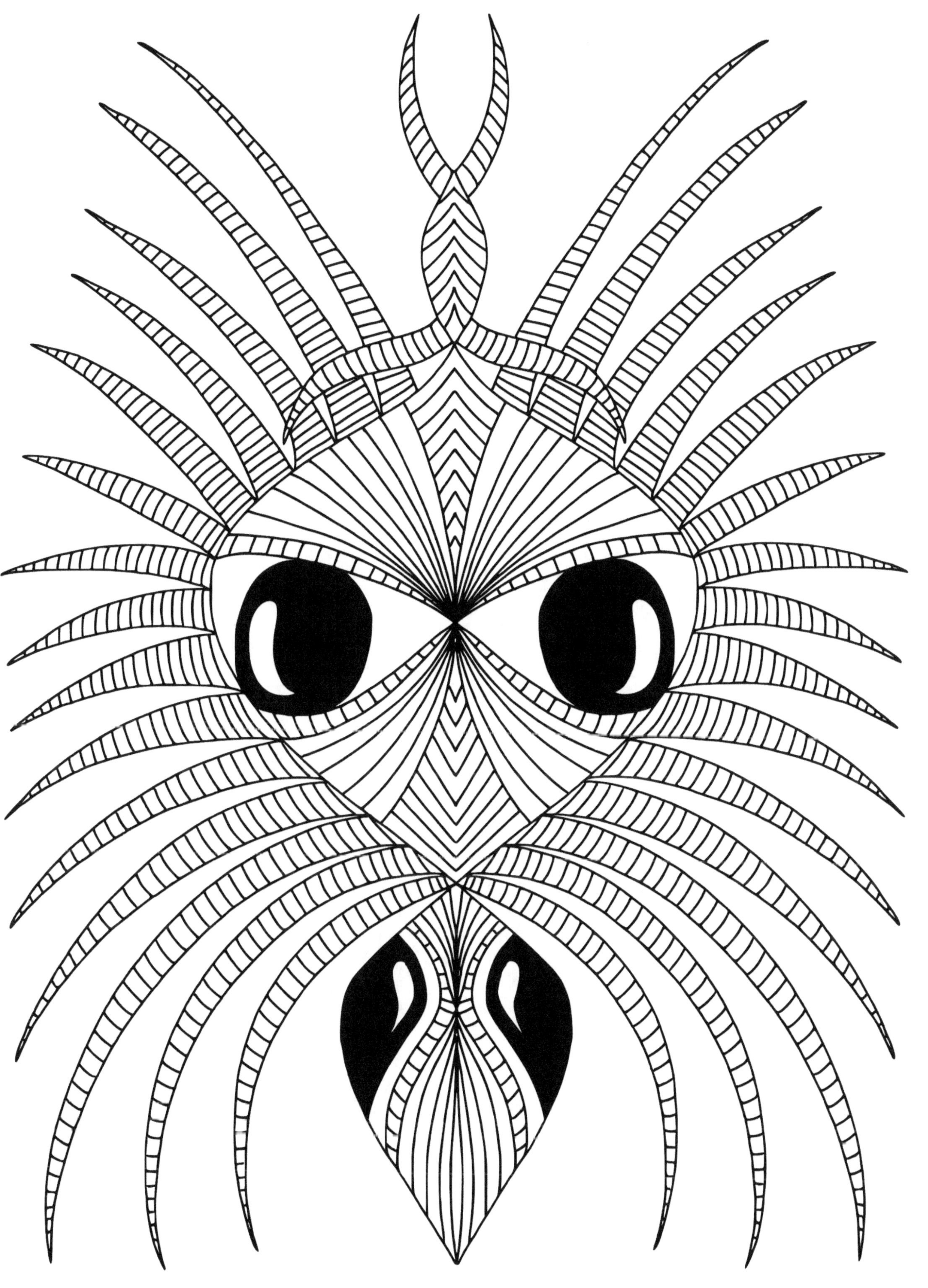

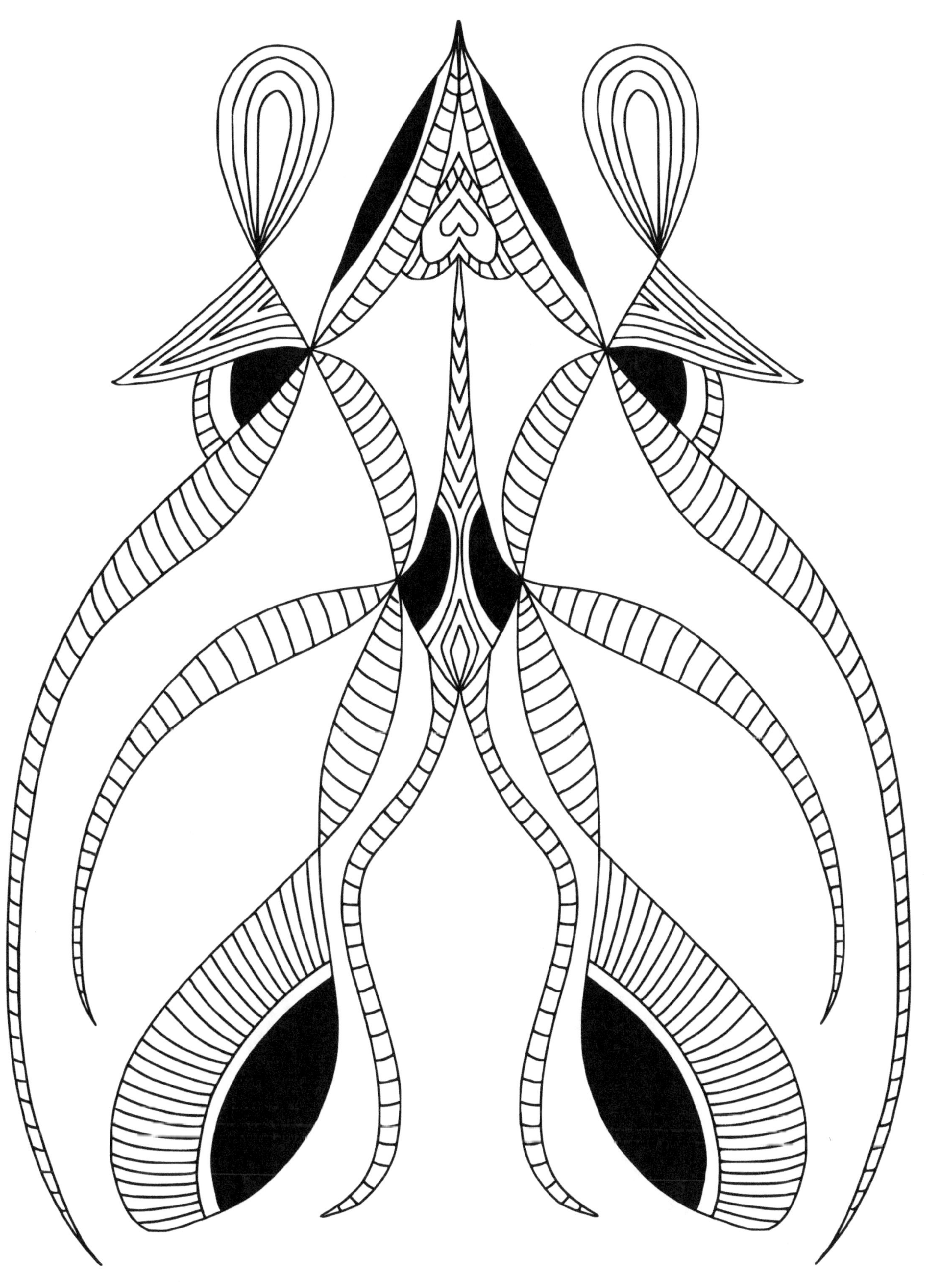

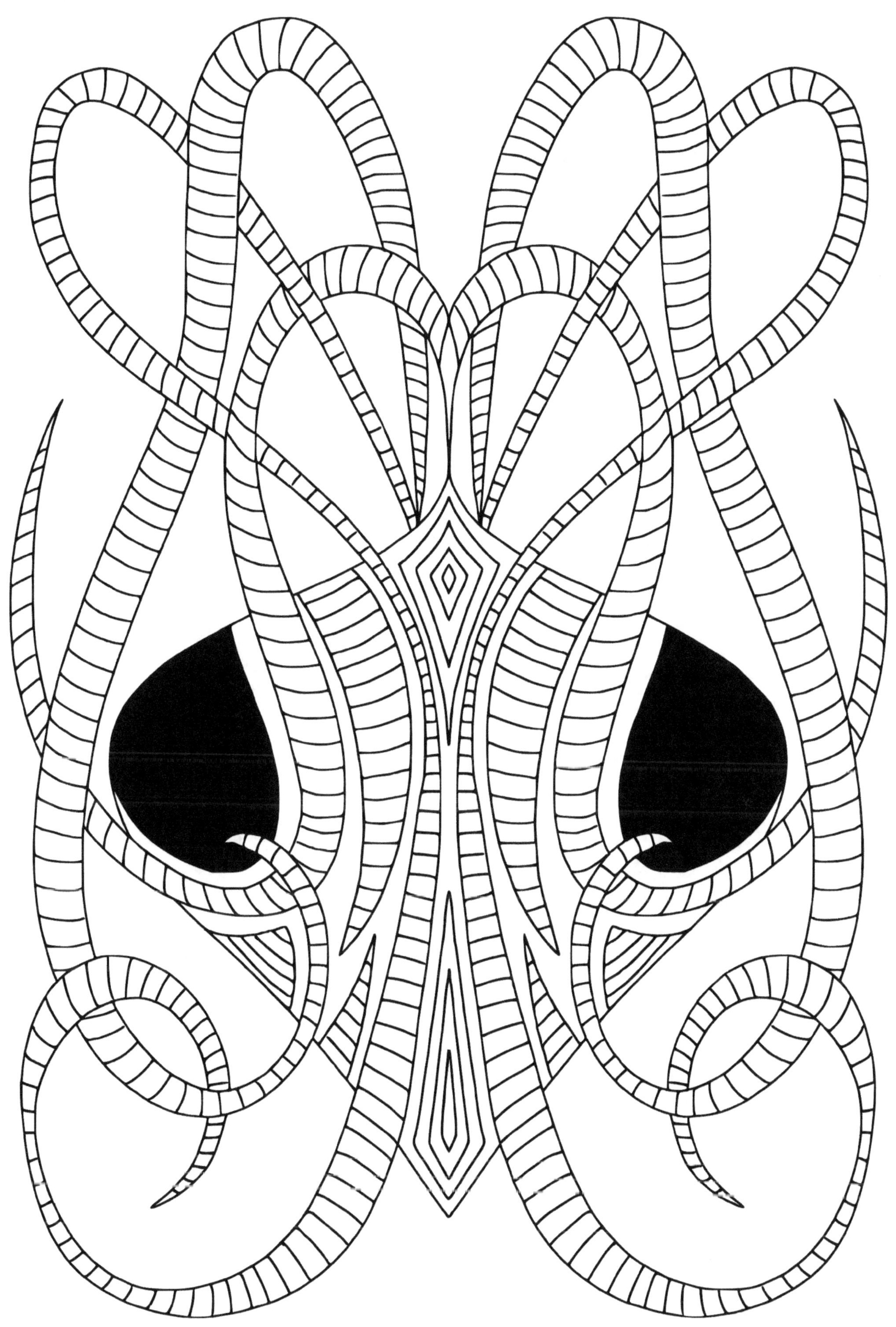

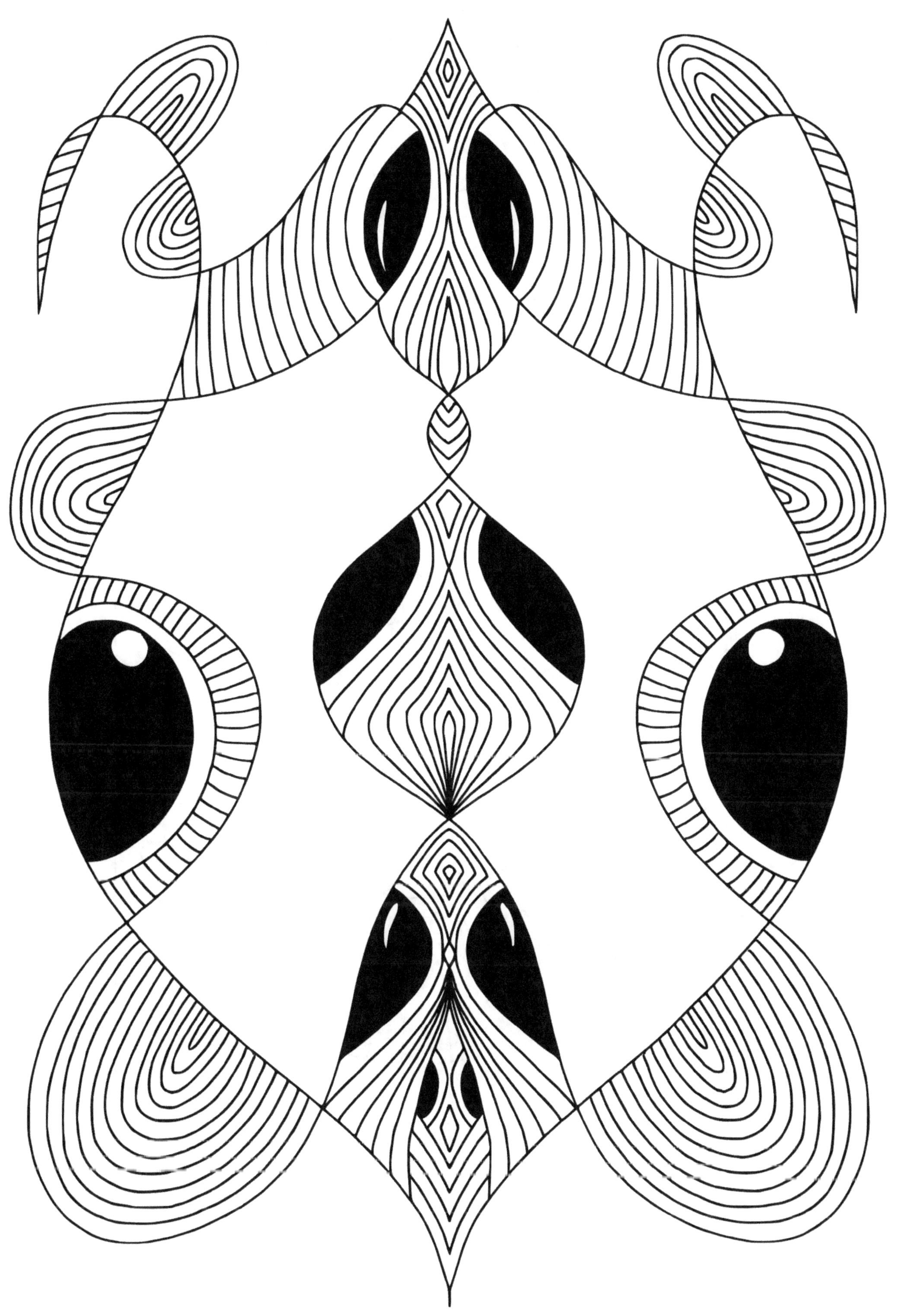

Test your colors here on the samples from
"My Pocket Coloring Companion"
&
"My Coloring Companion"

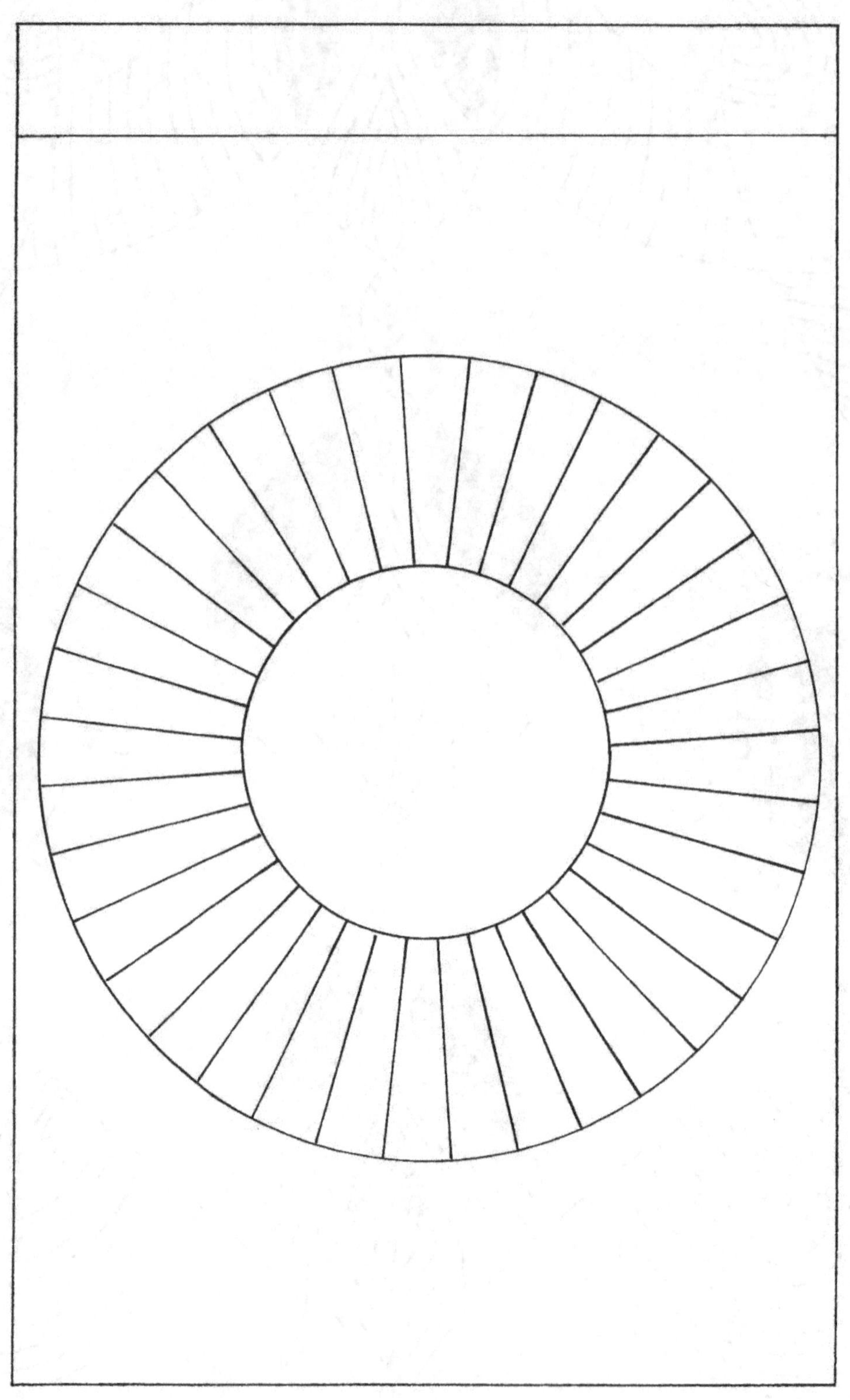

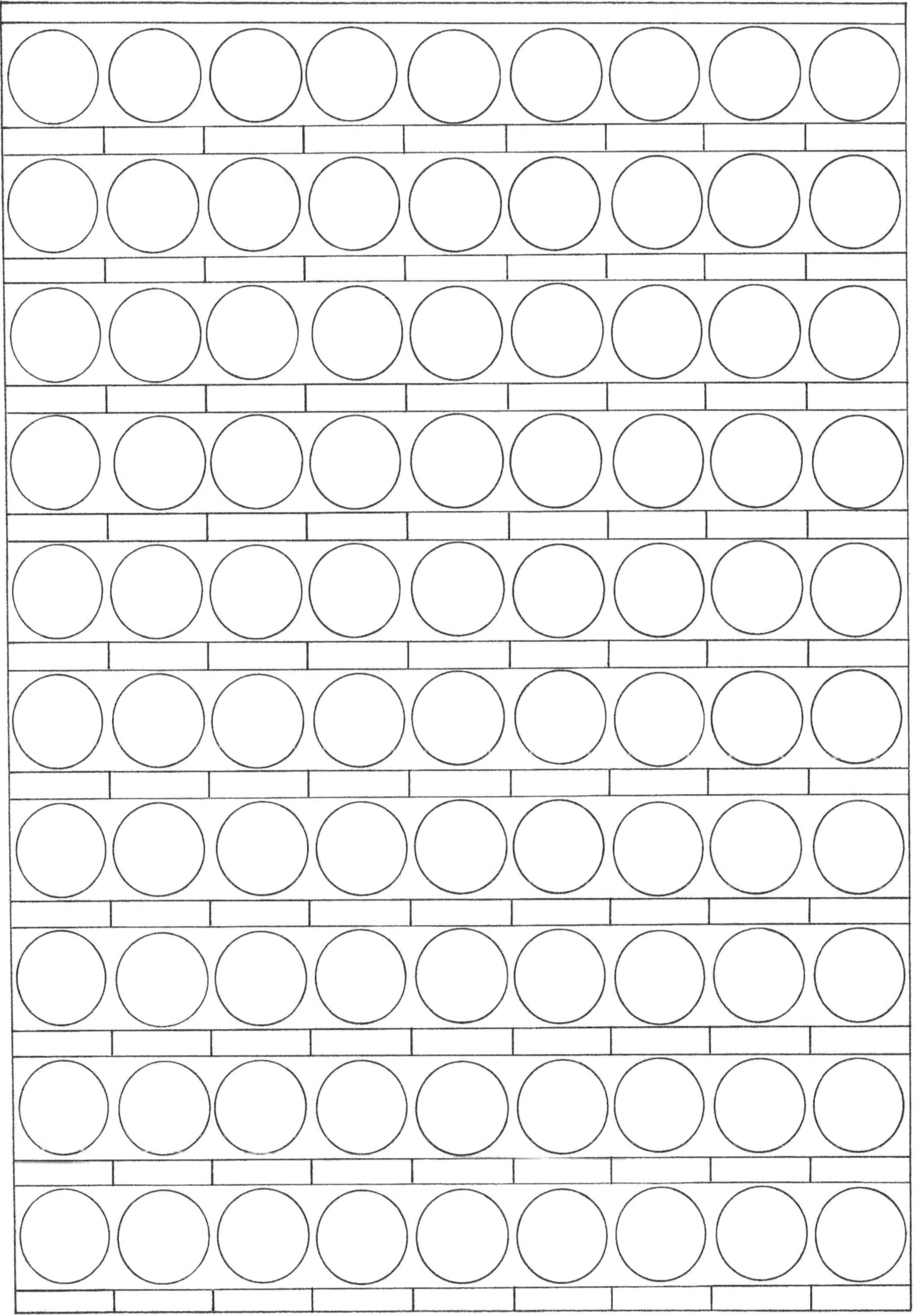